Praise for *The Amish Way*

"*The Amish Way* gives voice to the passion and purpose that inspires the Amish lifestyle and provides a clear description of their religious practices and spiritual identities. A must read for anyone who wants to understand Amish motivations."

—James A. Cates, Ph.D,.psychologist, founder of
the Amish Youth Vision Project

"What is Amish spirituality? The authors describe a way of life that puzzles outsiders and invite readers to sample the Amish wisdom of simplicity, patience, and community. Even if you do not want to trade in your car for a buggy, *The Amish Way* offers insights to all spiritual seekers for a more meaningful life in a fragmented world"

—Diana Butler Bass,author, *A People's History of
Christianity: The Other Side of the Story*

"Everything you wanted to know about Amish spirituality but were too busy to ask. This is a sympathetic and clear account, with a thoroughness that exceeds books three times its size."

—Rodney Clapp,author, *Johnny Cash and
the Great American Contradiction*

The Amish Way

OTHER BOOKS BY THE AUTHORS

Amish Grace: How Forgiveness Transcended Tragedy
Donald B. Kraybill, Steven M. Nolt,
David L. Weaver-Zercher

DONALD B. KRAYBILL

The Amish and the State (edited)
Amish Enterprise: From Plows to Profits (with Steven M. Nolt)
Anabaptist World USA (with C. Nelson Hostetter)
Concise Encyclopedia of Amish, Brethren, Hutterites, and Mennonites
On the Backroad to Heaven: Old Order Hutterites, Mennonites, Amish, and Brethren (with Carl Desportes Bowman)
The Riddle of Amish Culture

STEVEN M. NOLT

Amish Enterprise: From Plows to Profits (with Donald B. Kraybill)
An Amish Patchwork: Indiana's Old Orders in the Modern World (with Thomas J. Meyers)
Foreigners in Their Own Land: Pennsylvania Germans in the Early Republic
A History of the Amish
Mennonites, Amish, and the American Civil War (with James O. Lehman)
Plain Diversity: Amish Cultures and Identities (with Thomas J. Meyers)

DAVID L. WEAVER-ZERCHER

The Amish and the Media (edited with Diane Zimmerman Umble)
The Amish in the American Imagination
Vital Christianity: Spirituality, Justice, and Christian Practice (edited with William H. Willimon)
Writing the Amish: The Worlds of John A. Hostetler

The Amish Way

Patient Faith in a Perilous World

Donald B. Kraybill

Steven M. Nolt

David L. Weaver-Zercher

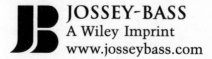
JOSSEY-BASS
A Wiley Imprint
www.josseybass.com

Published by Jossey-Bass
A Wiley Imprint
989 Market Street, San Francisco, CA 94103-1741—www.josseybass.com

Jossey-Bass books and products are available through most bookstores. To contact Jossey-Bass directly call
our Customer Care Department within the U.S. at 800-956-7739, outside the U.S. at 317-572-3986, or
fax 317-572-4002.

Jossey-Bass also publishes its books in a variety of electronic formats. Some content that appears in print
may not be available in electronic books.

All Scripture quotations are from the Holy Bible, King James version.

The Amish Lectionary found in Appendix II is printed with permission of Pathway Publishers from
In Meiner Jugend: A Devotional Reader in German and English, first printing in 2000, reprint 2008.
Translation by Joseph Stoll 1999.

Library of Congress Cataloging-in-Publication Data

Kraybill, Donald B.
    The Amish way : patient faith in a perilous world / Donald B. Kraybill, Steven M. Nolt, David
L. Weaver-Zercher.
        p.   cm.
    Includes bibliographical references and index.
    ISBN 978-0-470-52069-7 (hardback); 978-0-470-89087-5 (ebk); 978-0-470-89088-2 (ebk);
978-0-470-89097-4 (ebk)
        1. Amish. 2. Spirituality—Amish. I. Nolt, Steven M., date. II. Weaver-Zercher, David, date.
    III. Title.
    BX8121.3.K73   2010
    248.4'897—dc22
                                                                    2010021302

Printed in the United States of America
FIRST EDITION
HB Printing   10 9 8 7 6 5 4 3 2 1

CONTENTS

132 117

❦ Contents ❦

Part Four
Amish Faith and the Rest of Us   179

PREFACE

On October 2, 2006, the unthinkable took place in Lancaster County, Pennsylvania. On a crystal-clear Monday morning, a thirty-two-year-old milk truck driver armed with guns and ammunition entered a one-room Amish school. Embittered by the death of his infant daughter nine years earlier, he was determined to get even with God in a most gruesome way. After sending the boys out of the school, the gunman tied up the remaining children—ten girls, ages six through thirteen—and opened fire in execution style. Moments later, five girls lay dying, the rest had been seriously wounded, and the intruder had killed himself. One Amish leader, searching for words to describe the horror to his non-Amish neighbors, said simply, "This was our 9/11."

Although millions around the world were stunned that such evil could transpire in an Amish school, many were even more surprised when the Amish community, within hours, extended grace and forgiveness to the killer and his family. *How could anyone do what the Amish did, and do it as quickly as they did?*

This was the question we addressed in *Amish Grace: How Forgiveness Transcended Tragedy*. In writing that book, we interviewed dozens of Amish people and read scores of Amish publications, and we soon discovered that forgiveness is embedded more deeply in Amish life than we ever suspected. That realization inspired us to listen more closely for the religious heartbeat that sustains their entire way of life. This pulse, which often goes unnoticed, is more fundamental to the Amish way than the buggies and bonnets that receive so much attention. Strong but subtle, quiet yet persistent, this heartbeat is *Amish spirituality*.

One Braid, Three Strands

Defining spirituality is no easy task, but it involves at least three aspects: religious beliefs, practices, and affections.[1] By *religious beliefs* we mean how people understand and make sense of their world. Is the world inhabited by a supernatural power? If so, is this power a wise old man in the sky or a mysterious force in nature? Do angels wing their way through space to protect us, or does help arrive in more ordinary ways? Religious beliefs are sometimes expressed in logical, doctrinal statements, though many people find stories and images more helpful in articulating what they believe. Whatever form they take—creeds or parables, statements or stories—religious beliefs encompass what believers hold to be true.

These beliefs do not merely exist in people's minds, however. They take concrete shape through *religious practices*. Attending services, praying, singing, and helping others—these acts are more visible than beliefs but are tied to them in profound ways. In fact, religious practices both flow from and create religious beliefs. Consider the nonspiritual example of teeth-brushing. Parents make their children brush their teeth because they have strong views about oral hygiene and because they want their children to embrace those views. And although it may take many years, children who regularly brush their teeth will usually come to own their parents' beliefs on hygiene. Similarly, spiritual practices, both private and public ones, nurture a particular religious vision.

This vision generates *religious affections*, desires of the heart. All human beings have desires or impulses that drive them to act in certain ways. Most religions view some of these personal desires as misplaced, or at least out of balance. One of the chief aims of religion is to redirect people's affections, to help them desire the right things. In many religious traditions, including the Amish way, the primary goal is to nurture religious affections for God and the things that please God. Doing so often requires reducing desires for temporal things—perhaps even good ones.

Throughout this book we move back and forth among beliefs, practices, and affections. Sometimes we focus on Amish beliefs, sometimes on their practices, and other times on their affections. Ultimately, we see this trio as three strands of one braid that secures the entire Amish way. In other words, the spirituality of Amish people is not something that stands on its own, apart from their daily lives as mothers and fathers, farmers and carpenters, ministers and laypeople. Rather, their spirituality gives them a framework for making decisions about marriage, family, work, and play—indeed, a framework that helps them face all the pleasures and uncertainties that human life entails.

Patient Faith in a Perilous World

Most forms of spirituality promise resources for facing dangers. Whether these perils are physical, emotional, or moral, many people search earnestly for help beyond themselves. For many of them, this search leads to God, who according to the Judeo-Christian tradition is "a very present help in trouble" (Psalm 46:1). As Christians, the Amish look to God for help, even though, as we will see, some of the perils they seek to avoid are quite different from those identified by other Christians.

And Amish people demonstrate uncommon patience as they make their way in a perilous world. They do not skip from one thing to the next, but stick with traditional answers and approaches. When they are faced with problems, their first instinct is to wait and pray rather than seek a quick fix. Indeed, "the quick solution, the simple method, and the rapid cure" that characterize "our instant age" are dangerous, says one Amish church leader.[2] Demanding immediate solutions signals a lack of trust in God, and, in their view, patience is the best way to show acceptance of God's timing.

We find this commitment to patience fascinating and admirable, but also disconcerting. Although the three of us respect the religious views of the Amish on many levels, we have never been tempted to become Amish, in part because their patient approach runs counter to some of our deepest sensibilities. Is this much patience a good thing? What about working to change the world for the better? As Martin Luther King Jr. wrote in his book *Why We Can't Wait*, impatience is sometimes a virtue, for "progress never rolls in on wheels of inevitability."[3] Amish people are not patient in every way, of course, and they do nurture good even as they wait. Still, they reject the activist approach to tackling the world's problems. Activism—trying to change the world—is simply not the Amish way.

Although changing the world is not the Amish way, resisting the world is. All forms of spirituality are acts of resistance in some respect—resistance to despair or fear, for example—but most forms of spirituality do not resist the world as forcefully as the Amish do.

What the Amish seek to do, perhaps more than any religious community in North America, is to create a society in which members learn to resist the world's allures and desire the things of God. You could call it a counterculture of religious affection, but the Amish call it "separation from the world." It's a way of life based on the teachings of Jesus who, in his Sermon on the Mount, reminded his followers that no one can serve two masters. "Seek ye first the kingdom of God," Jesus said, and God will provide for your needs (Matthew 6:33). In other words, set your desires on spiritual priorities and you will have nothing to fear, even in a perilous world.

Looking Ahead

Rooted in the teachings of Jesus, Amish spirituality is a Christian vision, but one with a difference. In Part One of this book, "Searching for

Amish Spirituality," we highlight some distinctive aspects of their religious life, but also place it in the wider spectrum of Christianity.

In Part Two, "The Amish Way of Community," we explore the beliefs and practices that undergird the collective life of the Amish: giving up self-will, joining the church, worship and prayer, mutual aid, and church discipline. As we'll see, some of these spiritual practices are severe and uncompromising, reminding us that resistance always has a cost.

In "The Amish Way in Everyday Life," Part Three, we consider matters that face many humans—child rearing, family life, material possessions, the natural world, evil, and sorrow. For Amish people, these issues pose both problems and possibilities. We don't suggest that the Amish way is the best way to navigate these situations, but in Part Four we do ask, Is there anything the Amish can teach the rest of us about living meaningfully in the modern world? Although that question is complicated, we answer with a qualified yes.

We talked with a host of Amish people in the course of writing this book, and we quote many of them in the following pages. Because Amish culture emphasizes humility, the people we interviewed did not want their names to appear in print. We have respected their wishes and simply cite many of our sources as "an Amish mother," "an Amish minister," and so on. For the people we quote most often, we use typical Amish first names (Sadie, Reuben, Jesse) as pseudonyms. Each pseudonym refers to a real person, not a composite of several individuals. We have also assigned pseudonyms to some Amish authors who published their works anonymously. Otherwise we use the real names of Amish people who have already been identified in the mainstream media or use their own names when publishing articles, essays, or books for Amish readers. In the endnotes we cite the written sources we quote, but not the interviews.

It is risky to make sweeping statements about *the* Amish way of life, for there are some eighteen hundred individual congregations and over forty subgroups of Amish, and they have no central organization or governing body. The practices of these subgroups and local congregations vary in many ways. For example, reading habits and the amount of daily interaction with non-Amish neighbors vary, as does use of technology. Some households have indoor plumbing, cut their grass with gasoline-powered lawnmowers, and fasten LED lights to their buggies for night-time driving. Other congregations permit none of these things. Because we do not have space to examine these diverse details, we have focused on the most typical themes and practices.

The Amish Way

Part I

Searching for Amish Spirituality

CHAPTER ONE

A Peculiar Way

. . . in the Bible we find that God's people are to be peculiar.

—Amish leader[1]

Here's an idea for a slow Saturday night: ask your friends to
call out the first words they think of when you say the word
Amish. You might exhaust the usual suspects fairly quickly—
horses and buggies, bonnets and beards, barn raisings, quilts, and plain
clothes. Your group might settle on some adjectives: *gentle, simple, peace-
ful*, and *forgiving*. Then again, you might come up with words that lean
in another direction: *severe, harsh, judgmental*, and *unfriendly*. The range
of adjectives probably reflects the variety in Amish life—in any kind of
life, for that matter. More likely, however, the differences reflect your
point of view and the features of Amish life that capture your gaze.

Although the Amish are sometimes called a simple people, their
religious practices are often mystifying, and their way of life—like
all ways of life—is quite complex. It's no wonder outsiders hold con-
flicting views of the Amish, for the Amish are at once submissive and
defiant, yielding and yet unmoved. To use a common Amish phrase, one

we will explore more fully in later chapters, they are ready to "give up," but they do not readily give in.

These apparent paradoxes make the Amish hard to understand. They also make them enormously fascinating, the subjects of countless books, films, Web sites, and tourist venues.[2] In this chapter, we introduce some of the unique and distinctively religious elements of Amish society. We do this by offering nine vignettes illustrating aspects of Amish faith that rarely receive media attention but that nonetheless go to the heart of the Amish way. Together these stories demonstrate how the spirituality of Amish people leads them to do very intriguing—and what some would call very *peculiar*—things.

A Homespun Scholar

A few years ago we visited one of our Amish friends in Lancaster County, Pennsylvania, an older man who has since passed away. Abner was a bookbinder by trade, repairing the old or tattered books that people brought to him. He was also an amateur historian who founded a local Amish library. A warm and engaging person, Abner had many "English" (non-Amish) friends stopping by to visit.

One summer evening, sitting on lawn chairs, we talked about our families. "So where do your brothers and sisters live?" he asked, and we ran down the list: one lives near San Francisco, another in New Hampshire, and still another in northern Indiana. "Come with me," Abner said, and he led us around his house and into his backyard. His simple house backed up to the edge of a ridge, giving him an expansive view of farmland to the north. "Let me show you where my family lives," he said, pointing across the landscape. "My one sister lives there, and another right over there. And you see that road? I have five more relatives living along there." And with a sweep of his hand Abner showed us the homes of his fellow church members as well. "This is one of the things I like about being Amish," he said, and we stood quietly for a moment as we surveyed the fields and homes of his kin.

Abner didn't have to say more to make his message clear: the choices we had made as scholars, and the choices our siblings had made as professionals, had pulled our families apart, geographically and in other ways as well. Abner was a scholar too, of course, and we often asked him questions about Amish history. But his way of being a scholar didn't require moving across the country to pursue a Ph.D. In fact, pursuing that sort of life is forbidden for the Amish, who end their formal education at eighth grade.* Thus, for Abner, becoming a historian meant reading books in his spare time and asking lots of questions.

Abner clearly enjoyed talking with non-Amish people. Could it be that he lived vicariously through his educated non-Amish friends? Perhaps his backyard commentary that evening was a way of reminding himself, as well as us, that Amish life had its advantages. Still, if there was a message from that evening, it was this: our way of living, just like Abner's, comes at a cost.

Unwilling Warriors

In late 1953, two Amish men entered a federal courtroom in Des Moines, Iowa. Both in their early twenties, Melvin Chupp and Emanuel Miller showed up "wearing the beards and unbarbered hair traditional in their sect," according to the local newspaper.[3] A few hours later, they left with three-year prison terms for refusing to serve in the U.S. military.

---

*The Amish believe that eight grades of formal education, supplemented by vocational training, are sufficient to live a productive life. In 1972 the U.S. Supreme Court in *Wisconsin* v. *Yoder* permitted Amish people to end formal schooling at fourteen years of age. Appendix I provides more detail on Amish life and practice.

Melvin and Emanuel, like all members of their faith, viewed war as wrong and participation in it sinful. Although the federal government allowed war objectors to do alternate service outside the military, knowledge of this alternative apparently had not trickled down to the draft board in Buchanan County, Iowa. Rather than granting the two Amish men conscientious objector status, the draft board required them to do noncombatant service in the military. When Melvin and Emanuel refused that, the board ordered them into combat units. Once again they refused, which quickly led to their arrest.

At the trial, Melvin acted as his own attorney. His only statement came during closing arguments. He might have appealed to principles in the U.S. Constitution, but instead he focused on his Christian convictions. "Jesus never killed His enemies. He let his enemies kill Him," Melvin said. "Therefore, I'm here to *give myself up* to the jury." The judge who sentenced them to prison was not sympathetic. His only regret, he said, was that the two Amish men "found it impossible to accept noncombatant service." Melvin and Emanuel's decision to place faith above patriotism cost them three years of their lives.

A Church-First Businesswoman

Sadie is an enterprising businesswoman. In the early 1980s she started a dry goods store. Under her management, the business grew rapidly, adding new divisions and product lines and eventually selling everything from bulk foods to hardware. Sadie opened stores in several other locations, and altogether spawned eight retail businesses, including a shoe store and two grocery stores. Aware of her success, Sadie is nonetheless quick to deflect credit. "I think some people are just born with it," she told us. "I have this love of selling."

At first glance, her business model seems to track a Fortune 500 company: start a small business, expand into larger markets, reinvest the profits, and expand some more. But Sadie's story didn't follow that model. As an Amish businessperson, she faced restrictions. Her church frowns on members accumulating wealth or making "a big name for themselves." As one Amish person explained, "Bigness ruins everything."

So as Sadie's business grew, she sold off some of her product lines and stores to her employees, keeping her own holdings small. Sadie's plan spread the wealth and multiplied the number of owners within the Amish community.

Her decision to shrink her business did not come easily. She knew that she would earn less this way, and money was a concern for her family. In fact, she had first gone into business because she had special-needs children with significant medical costs. In the end, however, she concluded that the perils of growing her business and risking church censure were greater than the risks of downsizing.

A Reluctant Minister

Reuben is a thirty-two-year-old stonemason and father of three. He is also one of two ministers in his local congregation of about thirty families, but he never applied for the job or went to seminary. During a recent visit he explained how he had been selected by God to serve as a minister for the rest of his life.

As they hitched up their buggies and drove their families to church on the day of the ordination, Reuben and the other men in his congregation keenly felt the burden of knowing that they might be selected. Reuben explained that a man would never seek such a position and women are not eligible. Instead, by drawing lots, a method used by

7

Jesus' disciples to fill a vacancy in their ranks (Acts 1:12–26), the Amish believe that God miraculously selects ministers for them.*

We'll look more closely at this process in Chapter Four, but one of the most peculiar aspects to outsiders is that neither the nominees for the position nor the chosen one have the option to decline. When it suddenly became clear that he was selected, Reuben remembers having "a feeling of being between complete surrender and stepping out on the ice and not being sure how thick it was." The bishop immediately ordained Reuben for his new, lifelong position, and the entire process was over in less than ninety minutes.

During those minutes, the lives of Reuben and his family were changed forever. Reuben felt a heavy burden to help lead the congregation, and his family felt a new expectation to live exemplary Amish lives. Without the benefit of pay or formal training, and without the option to say no, Reuben soon began preaching sermons, counseling members, and helping resolve disputes—all in addition to his regular work as a mason. Rather than a time of celebration, an ordination is a somber, weighty occasion. "It's no 'Hurray!' type of thing," said a friend of Reuben's, a man who has been in the lot three times but never selected. "You would serve to the best of your ability if called, but you are also very grateful to take your usual seat again if another person is chosen."

A Self-Taught Artist

Susie Riehl, a Pennsylvania artist whose work can sell for more than $3,000, has never taken an art class. This Amish mother of five who paints watercolors featuring quilts, gardens, buggies, and barns is

---

*This procedure has traditionally been called *casting lots*; however, throughout the text we use the term *drawing lots* to describe the process.

finding ways to live within the constraints of her church while pursuing her artistic passions.

Although various types of folk art have long been accepted, the Amish church frowns on members showcasing their paintings at art shows, fearing it will lead to pride on the part of the artist. The church considers photographs and drawings of human faces taboo, a violation of the Second Commandment's prohibition of idols known as graven images (Exodus 20:4).

Susie honors the church's wishes by not appearing at public exhibitions of her artwork and by not drawing human faces. When children or even dolls appear in her work, they are faceless. "I don't want people to think I've lost my humility," she told a *USA Today* reporter. "I'm just working with a God-given talent and enjoying myself."[4]

A Would-Be Violinist

One of our friends, Nancy Fisher Outley, describes her Amish childhood as a happy time, especially the trips to town with her mother as she sold vegetables door-to-door. "I remember thoroughly enjoying those excursions, listening to my mother discuss an array of issues with her customers and friends," she says. Nancy felt "an overwhelming heaviness," however, when she entered the eighth grade, the end of formal schooling for Amish children.

Intentionally or not, Nancy's family had given her a "thirst for knowledge," fostered by books, magazines, and her mother's "keen curiosity and interest in world affairs." As a girl, she had fantasies about becoming a teacher or even a concert violinist. "I practiced a lot on my imaginary violin out behind the chicken house," she told us. Eventually she set her fantasies aside, and after finishing the eighth grade, started doing household work for her aunt. She was baptized into the Amish church, with what she calls "a very serious commitment," at the age of sixteen.

But her yearning for more education did not go away, and she soon did what very few Amish people do: she took eligibility exams and was admitted to college without a high school diploma. "I told my Amish bishop about my desire to go to college so that I could become a good teacher, and he reluctantly gave his approval." Eventually, however, her professional pursuits became public, and the bishop rescinded his permission. Because her pursuits violated church standards, she was excommunicated just before her senior year of college.

"This was a very painful experience," Nancy recalls, and describes meeting with her bishop a few days before her exit. "He was a deeply caring person," she says. "I asked questions about education and sin. . . . I wanted to continue both my education and membership in the Amish community. He would not say that further education was sin, and he agonized to explain why excommunication was necessary if I did not repent. Both of us were sensitive and hurt deeply. We cried unashamedly."

Nancy eventually received a master's degree and became a social worker. Unlike many ex-Amish people who feel deeply wounded, even embittered, by their community's decision to expel them, Nancy continues to have warm feelings toward the church of her youth. In fact, she credits some of her success as a social worker—her ability "to feel compassion and caring," as well as her commitment to straightforward communication—to her Amish roots. "Like my Amish bishop, I've been able to set limits for others with a great deal of caring and love so that the limits are not interpreted as rejection." [5]

A Retro Remodeler

Although articles and books about home improvement abound, Jesse, a forty-year-old father of six, needed remodeling knowledge of a different kind. Early in their married life, Jesse and his wife, Ruthie, bought a home on a three-acre plot of land. Jesse works in a furniture factory, so they didn't need much farmland, but he and Ruthie wanted a place with a barn and some pasture for their horses and enough acreage for a garden. This property fit the bill.

There was one problem, however: the previous owners were not Amish. This meant that Jesse and Ruthie had to "de-electrify" the house when they moved in to make it comply with church regulations. "The first thing we did was to begin using bottled-gas lights in our house," Jesse said. "This change announced, 'This is an Amish home.'" They also hooked up a propane-powered refrigerator and stove to gas lines connected to a propane tank outside.* Other changes followed until finally they faced their biggest issue: the electric water pump. "That was the hardest thing for me," Jesse confessed.

The electricity to run the water pump cost only $15 per month, but Jesse and Ruthie had to pay $14,000 to install a small diesel engine to replace the electric pump. The diesel engine creates pneumatic (air) power to operate their water pump, washing machine, and Ruthie's sewing machine. Their propane refrigerator cost twice as much as an electric one, said Jesse. In fact, "it would have been cheaper for us to stay electric."

The de-electrification process took about four years. "Our ministers were very understanding," Jesse said. "The main thing was to be headed in the nonelectric direction," a direction that signaled to fellow church

---

*In lieu of electricity, the Amish use other types of energy to power household appliances. See Chapter Nine and Appendix I for more detail.

members that Jesse's family took the church's rules seriously. Today the shell of an electric meter remains visible on the outside of their brick farmhouse, but it hasn't carried any current for years.

A Family That Accepts Death

Elam was an eighteen-year-old carpenter. One Wednesday morning, he fell from a roof and suffered serious head injuries. An ambulance rushed him to a nearby hospital, where medical staff placed him on a respirator and conducted tests to decide treatment. Within two days, however, the attending doctor determined that Elam's brain was not functioning. His family, though grieving deeply, decided that they wanted to release him into God's loving hands and cease medical intervention.

Trained to view death as defeat, the hospital staff resisted removing the respirator. Finally, on the following Monday, the family prevailed on the hospital to disconnect the machine. Elam's breathing ceased, and doctors declared him dead.

"You will note that the obituary published in the Lancaster newspaper says that he died on Monday," an Amish church member noted later, but "the time of death . . . was announced at the funeral as having been on Friday." The Amish did not believe that a body forced to breathe by a machine was a living person, despite the insistence of medical professionals. "The truth was that his soul had fled," a family friend explained.[6]

A Compassionate Community

In February 2007, a twenty-eight-year-old Amish schoolteacher named Leah King was making her way along a narrow road to the one-room school where she taught Amish children. Leah lived less than a mile

from the school, and she walked to work almost every day. This particular morning was cold and icy, and Leah was struck by a pickup truck
that hit a patch of ice and slid out of control. She died at the scene.[7]

Although grief-stricken by the death of their daughter, sister, and
friend, many Amish people also understood the heartache of the driver,
Earl Wenger, and his family. Shortly after the accident, the King family
invited the Wenger family to attend Leah's viewing, which in Amish
fashion took place in a home. When the Wengers arrived for the viewing, an Amish woman urged them to sit with the other mourners. "Most
persons . . . who passed by us extended their hands to shake ours,"
recalls Wenger's daughter, who accompanied her parents. One Amish
woman told Earl Wenger, "It's not your fault. It was God's will." When
Wenger's wife asked her name, she answered, "I am Leah's mother."

A week later, an Amish newspaper carried a letter written by
Leah's mother urging Amish people across the country to "keep him [Earl
Wenger] in our thoughts and prayers." She also included Wenger's mailing
address, in case "anyone would like to send a few lines his way."[8]

In response the Wengers received over eighty sympathy cards,
many of them addressed to "Dear Unknown Friends" or "Dear Ones."
Each note was different, but the sentiments were always the same, full
of compassion and concern. One note came from a fifteen-year-old
Amish girl who, in the course of two pages, told the Wengers about the
weather, her family members, and the joy of making maple syrup.
She added, "I can only imagine how you must feel. But please don't
blame yourself. Accidents do happen sometimes."[9]

A Peculiar People

Few Amish people would find the preceding stories remarkable. Non-Amish
readers, however, might understand why the Amish have sometimes

been labeled "a peculiar people."[10] These unusual stories—and we could add many more—suggest that peculiar is an apt description.

To call something peculiar implies departing from a benchmark, in this case the dominant values of modern life—which, we might add, the *Amish* find quite peculiar. In mainstream society, desires for wealth, choice, status, justice, and personal acclaim run very high, so high that they sometimes jeopardize people's health, their families, and their friendships. Most people rarely question these values; in fact, even recognizing them can be difficult.

Amish people are surely not peculiar or countercultural in every way. With few exceptions they believe in free-market capitalism, political democracy, and conservative family values. They value meaningful work, enjoy leisure, prefer pleasure over pain, marry for love, treasure their children, and grieve the loss of loved ones. On many fronts, however, the Amish do resist mainstream culture and challenge dominant assumptions about the good life. Some symbols of their resistance—horses and buggies, for example—are easy to spot. But such visible signs of Amish life stand on deep assumptions about contentment and the meaning of life.

The Amish don't talk much about resistance. They are much more likely to speak about "obedience to God" or "separation from the world," phrases that remind them that God-fearing people often find themselves out of step with the larger society. They also use the term *uffgevva*, a Pennsylvania German word that literally means "to give up," to describe their rejection of self-centeredness. In other words, Amish resistance springs from their willingness to give themselves up to God and to the church.

Although media images of the Amish may conjure notions of Buddhist-like nirvana in which selfish desires have been overcome, Amish people don't talk about their lives that way. For them, the giving-up process—yielding themselves to God's will and submitting to the church's expectations——is a lifelong struggle. It begins in childhood, ends at death, and punctuates many moments in between. A day rarely passes when an Amish person doesn't feel the need to give himself or herself up to God and community.

Giving up is not easy, even for committed Amish people. "Hen nature and human nature have a great deal in common," writes one Amish farmer-theologian; human beings, like chickens, would rather be free to do as they please. Nonetheless, he continues, "true contentment is found in submission and obedience and in seeking God's will."[11]

This writer's claim, deeply rooted in Amish spiritual resources, shapes a host of Amish practices. Many of those resources, reaching back some four hundred years, are found on the bookshelves of Amish homes, as we will see in the next chapter.

CHAPTER TWO

Spiritual Headwaters

Christ is our fortress, *patience* our weapon of defense . . .

—ANABAPTIST LEADER (1539)[1]

Walk into an Amish home and you may find a hefty book sitting on a bookshelf or end table. *Our Heritage, Hope, and Faith* spans almost six hundred pages and weighs four solid pounds.[2] Even more striking than its size are the large Gothic letters across its front cover and down its fat spine. The Gothic English mirrors the traditional German script in the Bibles used by Amish people. In fact, were you to open *Our Heritage, Hope, and Faith*, you'd find a two-column format of German text alongside an English translation.

Mary M. Miller, an Amish woman in Indiana, compiled the volume to provide her people easy access to prayers, songs, and scripture readings used in their worship and devotional life. What is interesting about this distinctly Amish book is just how ordinarily Christian it is. The table of contents sounds familiar to Christian ears. It begins with "Holy Bible," then moves on to "Prayers," "Church," "Baptism," "Communion," and similar topics. Lengthy Bible passages appear at many points, and the prayers frequently address "our beloved heavenly Father" or "the Lord Jesus Christ." The English text recalls the King James Version of the Bible, with "thees" and "thous" sprinkled throughout. *Our Heritage, Hope, and Faith* may seem old-fashioned, but it is unmistakably a Christian book.

And that is a key point: *Amish spirituality is a form of Christian spirituality*. Shortly after the Nickel Mines shooting, we asked an Amish carpenter to explain Amish forgiveness. Puzzled at first by our question, he paused and said, "It's just standard Christian forgiveness, isn't it?"

Generic Christians?

The carpenter's response speaks volumes about how the Amish understand their spirituality. For them, the Amish way is simply the Christian way, begun by Jesus Christ and carried forward by his followers.[3] They worship the triune God (Father, Son, and Holy Spirit); affirm the life, death, and resurrection of Jesus Christ, who alone can save them from sin and death; and view the devil as their adversary. They believe that the Old and New Testaments of the Bible are the written word of God with spiritual truths to be learned and obeyed. Every Amish home has at least one German Bible, most also have an English one, and many have an Amish-published edition with Martin Luther's German translation alongside the King James English text.[*]

Not surprisingly then, *Our Heritage, Hope, and Faith* begins with a lengthy section on the Bible, which Miller notes is "the traveler's map,

---

*Throughout this book, we quote from the 1611 King James Version of the Bible in order to provide readers with the wording that is commonly used by Amish people when they read the Bible in English.

the pilgrim's staff, the pilot's compass, the soldier's sword, and the Christian's charter." The scriptures, she says, should "fill the memory, rule the heart, and guide the feet" of every Amish person. More than any other text, the Bible shapes the Amish way and those who walk it.[4]

Clearly the headwaters that feed the streams of Amish spirituality are found in the hills of historic Christianity. Yet the Amish are not generic Christians. They have a distinctive understanding of the Christian faith that is found in several historical texts. *Our Heritage* includes excerpts from these sources, which we explore later in this chapter.

We start, however, five hundred years ago, when the Amish story began. It's a story of a small band of feisty Christians who resisted the ruling ideas about faith and who were, as a result, harassed, tortured, and even killed.

Heretics and Infidels

Western Europe was a religious monopoly at the beginning of the sixteenth century. The Roman Catholic Church, under the authority of the pope, was basically the only religious option in town. Belonging to it assured people of receiving God's saving grace, and infant baptism was a key ritual that incorporated everyone into the church. Ordinary people and church authorities alike agreed that salvation could not be found outside the Catholic Church. For this reason, and also because it was the law, most parents were eager to have their infants baptized by the local Catholic priest.

The monopoly was shattered by the Protestant Reformation, which began in 1517 and produced an array of Christian groups. One of the most radical movements to appear, and the one that eventually spawned the Amish church, was *Anabaptism*. The Anabaptist movement began around 1525, when a group of young reformers rebelled against

19

the infant baptism practiced in both Protestant and Catholic churches. These upstarts argued that the New Testament taught that baptism was only appropriate for adults who were willing to obey Jesus' teachings, and then they promptly began baptizing one another. When word of what they were doing got around, the group was sarcastically labeled *Anabaptists*, or *rebaptizers*. To those who disliked them, the Anabaptists' second baptism didn't count for anything. For the Anabaptists, however, the baptism of adult believers who voluntarily chose to follow the teachings of Christ was the only one that mattered.

Because they baptized adults and rejected infant baptism, Anabaptists were considered heretics and infidels. Seen as radicals who challenged the very foundations of the established church and government, they were hunted down and captured. Many were tortured, burned at the stake, or executed.

For the next two hundred years, other Christians viewed the Anabaptist movement as dangerous for several reasons. First, the Anabaptists declared that the Bible, particularly the words of Jesus, trumped the church's long-standing traditions and the laws of civil government. Officials feared the worst if they let these political subversives rely on the words of Jesus to undercut the laws of the land. Second, the Anabaptist refusal to baptize infants struck some as spiritually dangerous—placing their children's salvation at risk. Moreover, the government needed baptismal records to keep track of citizenship, calculate taxes, and manage inheritance law. Without infant baptism, officials feared, civil chaos would ensue.

All in all, the decision to rebaptize meant choosing a perilous life. The number of Anabaptists who died for their faith eventually exceeded two thousand. Although these spiritual ancestors of the Amish looked like heretics in their time, they were laying the foundation for what many people today take for granted: the separation of church and state and government-sanctioned religious freedom.

Lingering Marks of Martyrdom

Persecution of Anabaptists eventually came to an end, but not before it had profoundly shaped the movement. Early Anabaptists concluded that faithful Christians would inevitably find themselves at odds with the larger world. One early Anabaptist statement even claimed that all of humanity fell into one of two camps: good (Anabaptist Christians) or evil (everyone else).[5] Later Anabaptists would soften this divide, but they still were suspicious of the larger world and its spiritual perils.

Even today, many Anabaptists—Amish, Mennonites, and others— find the phrase "separation from the world" a useful way to articulate their values and commitments. An Amish handbook on the Christian life couldn't be clearer: "Know ye not that friendship with the world is enmity with God? Whosoever . . . will be a friend of the world is the enemy of God."[6] Being wary of the world and keeping some distance from it are central to Amish faith, and they have practical implications for such matters as clothing and the use of technology.

Persecution compelled many Anabaptists toward pacifism, also called *defenselessness* or *nonresistance*. Simply put, they had to choose how to respond to their persecutors: fight back in some way, or forgo the use of violence, even in self-defense. Early Anabaptist history reveals various responses, but the pacifist one soon became dominant.

Swayed by Jesus' nonviolent example and his teachings in the Sermon on the Mount (Matthew 5–7), Anabaptists chose not to resist evil with force. This response often brought physical suffering. One Anabaptist leader wrote that his people armed themselves only with spiritual weapons because "Christ is our fortress, *patience* our weapon of defense, and the Word of God our sword." True Christians will leave "iron and metal spears and swords to those who regard human blood and swine's blood about alike."[7]

21

Resisting the world's allures and forgoing violence, even in the face of persecution, have never been easy. The Amish find inspiration in a massive and revered book, *The Bloody Theatre, or Martyrs Mirror of the Defenseless Christians*, known simply as *Martyrs Mirror*.[8] First published in 1660 by a Dutch Anabaptist minister, the thousand-page *Martyrs Mirror* contains stories of over eight hundred Anabaptist martyrs. These stories detail midnight arrests, inquisitions at the hands of governing authorities, and gruesome executions.

The martyrs do not fight back. Some even ask God to forgive those who persecute them, much as Jesus did when he was nailed to the cross (Luke 23:34). The story of Dirk Willems saving his captor's life is particularly well known in Amish circles. A Dutch Anabaptist imprisoned in 1569, Willems escaped from his cell and fled across a frozen moat. He made it safely across, but the guard pursuing him fell through the ice and would have drowned. Not wanting the man to die, Willems turned around and pulled his pursuer to safety, saving his life. For his kindness, Dirk Willems was rearrested and promptly executed.

Today, 350 years later, *Martyrs Mirror* remains an important book in Amish life. It's a popular gift for newly married couples, and many Amish families pass along copies from generation to generation. One Amish publisher sells several hundred *Martyrs Mirror*s each year in both German and English.[9] *Martyrs Mirror* is not the kind of book one reads from cover to cover. Its oversized pages are filled with tiny print, and its prose is dense and difficult.

Amish people do read the book, however, and ponder its 104 illustrations during family or private devotions. Some of the pictures are chilling, such as one titled "The burning of eighteen persons in Salzburg in 1528," complete with flames and billowing smoke. Other etchings are dramatic in their poignancy, such as a scene showing a young mother handing over her infant son to be raised by someone else as she is led out of town to be executed for her faith.

An Amish woman recalls that she and her siblings would crowd onto her father's lap while he sat in his rocking chair and held *Martyrs Mirror* open for all to see. "We would look at all the pictures, one by one, and Dad would tell the story to each picture," she told us. "We never tired of hearing the stories even if we knew them by heart."[10]

Many non-Amish parents would think twice before exposing their young children to bone-chilling stories of atrocities that end in death. Amish children do sometimes find them frightening; our source told us that she remembers "many times sitting in church and wondering how it would be if the [building] were set on fire." But for Amish readers, these stories depict the courage to suffer for Christ's sake, to live faithfully, and to die well. Such accounts also shape a distinctive identity and give Amish people a sense of being part of something much greater than just themselves.

Amish Birth Pangs

Although the outside threat made the group more cohesive, the early Anabaptists didn't agree on everything. Eventually some of these disagreements festered into a division, and in 1693, a group of Anabaptists in Switzerland and France, led by Jakob Ammann, formed their own movement. Called *Ammanists* at first, the group later assumed the name *Amish*. About fifty years later, they began moving to North America in pursuit of both religious toleration and economic opportunity. This is where they continue to live out their unique form of Christian spirituality.*

What spawned this new Anabaptist subgroup? Historians offer several explanations, but the bottom line is this: the Amish felt that their Swiss Anabaptist counterparts had strayed from the original Anabaptist

*Appendix I provides more detail on Amish history, population, and contemporary life.

vision. Ammann complained that other Anabaptists had grown too friendly with the world and were too lax in their lifestyles. Worse yet, he felt, was that his fellow church leaders had abandoned biblical teachings on *avoidance* (also known as *shunning*). Ammann argued that church members who persistently disobeyed church rules should not merely be excluded from the Lord's Supper (Holy Communion, or the Eucharist) but also be treated as outsiders until they repented. The Amish views on these points, writes one historian, ensured "a sharper sense of separation from the world and reflected their desire to maintain the purity of the church."[11]

That issue—church purity—stands at the center of two sections of the Dordrecht Confession of Faith, a seventeenth-century Anabaptist document the Amish still regard as their doctrinal standard and use to instruct baptismal candidates.[12] In fact, these two sections on church discipline may be the reason that the confession remains at the head-waters of Amish spirituality. Even today the Amish uphold the form of church discipline—excommunication, followed by shunning—that Jakob Ammann advocated and for which the Dordrecht Confession provides a rationale. This practice, which we'll dissect in Chapter Six, sets the Amish apart from other Anabaptist groups.

But the Dordrecht Confession is not exclusively Amish; it also summarizes themes that are key for other Anabaptist groups. For example, it reserves baptism for adult believers, notes that Jesus forbids "all revenge and retaliation," and calls for high ethical standards based on his life. Adult baptism, pacifism, and Christian discipleship constitute the core of the Anabaptist tradition, which the Amish embrace fully.[13]

The confession's contents also show that the Amish swim in the stream of conventional Christianity. Its eighteen sections (it's often dubbed the "Eighteen Articles" by Amish people) includes articles on such basic Christian beliefs as God, human sinfulness, the significance of Jesus Christ, repentance, the church, and God's final judgment.

Amish faith, then, is best understood as a particular type of Christianity and, more specifically, a particular type of Anabaptist Christianity. And just as the Dordrecht Confession expresses both the uniqueness of the Amish faith and its affinities with other Christian traditions, so too do Amish songs and prayers, many of which date back to the early Anabaptist movement.

Time-Tested Songs and Prayers

Unless you know German and can read Old Gothic type, you might be baffled while paging through a copy of the *Ausbund*, the only hymnal used in Amish church services.[14] Its 140 hymns were largely written in the sixteenth and early seventeenth centuries, in the midst of severe persecution. *Ausbund* hymns frequently refer to martyrdom and the importance of remaining steadfast in times of trial. In fact, some of the hymns were composed by Anabaptists who were in prison and awaiting execution.

More than merely recounting the horrors of persecution, however, the *Ausbund* teaches worshipers about the nature of the Christian faith, and the demands and rewards of following Christ. One hymn, translated from the German, says:

> The Father we will praise, who has redeemed us,
> In Heaven on high, through his Son's death,
> Whom he has given to make atonement for our sin,
> That we might live in faith as his obedient child. . . .
> Whoever truly lays hold of God's word and believes in his heart,
> Hating all sin and malice, to him the [reward] is granted.[15]

These blood-stained hymns anchor Amish people in the faith of their spiritual ancestors, women and men who heeded God's call in the most perilous circumstances.

Like their hymns, Amish prayers have a long history. In contrast to many Christians who compose their prayers as they say them, the Amish rely primarily on written prayers in a book titled *Die Ernsthafte Christenpflicht* (The Prayer Book for Earnest Christians). First published in the early 1700s, the prayer book's resources are only slightly more contemporary than the hymns of the *Ausbund*.[16] The collection, written in German by both Anabaptist and non-Anabaptist authors and intended for private devotional reading, includes prayers for morning and evening, a prayer for "devout parents for their children," a traveler's prayer, a pre-sermon prayer, and "a reminder of several points for which we should rightly sigh and pray to God." *Christenpflicht* is now used by the Amish in church services and for family devotions. For the Amish, these prayers are second in importance only to the Lord's Prayer, the model prayer that Jesus taught (Matthew 6:9–13).

The continued use of these three spiritual fountains—the Dordrecht Confession, the *Ausbund*, and *Christenpflicht*—sets the Amish apart from other North American Christians, including most of their Anabaptist counterparts. Along with the Bible and *Martyrs Mirror*, these texts feed the headwaters of Amish spirituality. Given the high regard the Amish have for their heritage, it is not surprising that Mary Miller drew heavily from these five sources when she compiled *Our Heritage, Hope, and Faith*.

Rick Warren Enters the Mix

Although firmly anchored in Anabaptism, the Amish way also finds direction from other sources, especially a devotional book that originated in eighteenth-century Lutheran circles. *Lust Gärtlein* includes prayers for everyday life and for major church holidays.[17] Interestingly, some of the *Lust Gärtlein* prayers run against the grain of Anabaptist theology. In fact, a few even mention infant baptism, which prompts the question: Why have the Amish grown so attached to this book?

The answer lies in the book's opening section, "Rules of a Godly Life," which provides forty-seven rules for directing one's thoughts, words, and deeds.* "Beloved friend," it begins, "if you desire to lead a holy and God-pleasing life, . . . then you must measure your whole life by the Word of God as the only standard of faith and conduct, and let all your thoughts, words, and deeds be in accord with the same."

Several dozen specific instructions follow. "In the morning, awake with God and consider that this might be your final day," directs the first rule on guiding one's thoughts. A few pages later, readers are given instructions for bedtime: "Never go to sleep without first reviewing how you have spent the day just past, what you have accomplished for good or evil, and you will readily perceive whether or not you are making good use of your time." Rule ten for governing one's words offers this advice: "Make a habit of not replying to the words of others or to pass judgment unless you have first listened and understood well what they are saying to you."[18]

As with *Christenpflicht*, the use of *Lust Gärtlein* tells us that Amish people are quite willing to use spiritual resources developed by other Christians. One section of *Our Heritage, Hope, and Faith* includes popular prayers and devotional snippets from a range of non-Amish authors. For instance, "One Solitary Life," the anonymous poem about Jesus' remarkable influence, takes up two pages, and comes right before the widely quoted Serenity Prayer, written by twentieth-century American theologian Reinhold Niebuhr. Another page, titled "Desiderata," quotes a long poem that tells readers to "go placidly amid the noise and haste, and remember what peace there may be in silence."[19]

---

*The complete text of "Rules of a Godly Life" appears in Appendix III.

27

The non-Amish resources in *Our Heritage* are at least fifty years old, but many Amish people draw spiritual strength from more up-to-date resources as well. Our Amish friend Jesse, describing sources preachers use to prepare sermons, listed some contemporary evangelical works: books by Max Lucado, as well as apologetic works like Lee Strobel's *The Case for Christ*.[20] He also estimated that about half of his friends under age forty (including himself) have read Rick Warren's best-selling devotional treatise *The Purpose Driven Life*.[21] We were curious whether Jesse liked the book. "The first half is good," he said, especially Warren's admonition that "it's not about you," which reflects an Anabaptist theme.

Jesse reads more widely than most Amish church members, but his reading shows that Amish people find inspiration in the broader Christian tradition. They share spiritual resources with many other Christians, from the New Testament to certain old Lutheran prayers, from Reinhold Niebuhr to Rick Warren, and they gladly borrow what they find useful. At the same time, the Amish are Christians with a difference, shaped by their peculiar history and the resources bestowed by their spiritual ancestors. In the next four chapters we explore how the Amish way finds expression in the religious life of their communities.

Part II

The Amish Way of Community

CHAPTER THREE

Losing Self

Humility Is the Most Beautiful Virtue

—Title of an Amish hymn

Although few of us have lives like those of the folks in Western genre novels and films, many Americans are fond of Westerns and the ideals they extol. You know the story line: a town faces a problem it cannot solve. Just in time, a lone rider appears on the horizon to set things right. Only a solo operator—a true lone ranger who answers to no one but himself—can save the community. He does, and the townspeople are grateful. They may even ask the hero to stay, although deep down they know that he can't. Were he to join a community and become accountable to others, his heroic qualities would vanish. Having saved the day, the solitary savior rides away—either on to his next mission or straight into that ever-present sunset.[1]

So what do Westerns have to do with the Amish? Very little, other than that these stories throw into sharp relief the chasm between popular American values and those that the Amish hold dear. By glancing at the themes of Westerns, we can see more clearly who the Amish are not—and, in the process, learn more about who they are. Far from having a lone ranger–style spirituality, the Amish submit themselves and their spiritual pursuits to others at almost every turn.

Sheilaism

The Western is only one of many all-American stories that celebrate the individual. From superstar athletes to Wall Street risk-takers to people who achieve up-by-their-bootstraps success, America loves heroes who act alone, exude self-confidence, and refuse to conform. Even when advertisers entice consumers to buy the same things that everyone else is buying, they appeal to personal choice and the promise that their products will help buyers create a unique identity. There are exceptions to this pattern, of course. Plenty of people join communities and form long-lasting bonds, and many more wax nostalgic about bygone neighborhoods where people knew one another's names. But the cultural tide pulls strongly toward those who are mobile and unattached, and nostalgia only goes so far. If we don't actually worship the individual, we certainly admire the unfettered life.

This independent streak also shapes American religious life. Sociologist Robert Bellah illustrates this impulse with the story of Sheila Larson, a woman he interviewed for his book *Habits of the Heart.* Sheila was a young nurse who believed in God, but had developed her own faith and named it after herself: Sheilaism. "I can't remember the last time I went to church," Sheila admitted to Bellah, but "my faith has carried me a long way. It's Sheilaism. Just my own little voice." Although Sheila was unusual in having named her personal faith, her brand of solo spirituality was common among people Bellah interviewed across the country.[2] Contemporary spirituality is highly individual and deeply private: no one else can judge the authenticity or integrity of this sort of faith. Like the lone ranger, it answers to no one.

Where Everybody Knows Your Name (and More)

The Amish would find Sheilaism impossible to comprehend. Like other aspects of their lives, spirituality is a community affair. If you are an Amish adult, you have been baptized in the presence of two hundred or more relatives and neighbors. At some point in your life, you may need to openly confess sin in front of the same people. Your church decides how you must dress and when your formal education ends. Having a driver's license or owning a microwave are religious matters on which the church has the final word. Only rarely would your teachers have encouraged individual creativity, and your parents would never have urged you to be whatever you want to be. Instead, you would have been taught that deep meaning and enduring contentment can best be found in community.

This level of community comes with a great deal of security. A mother knows that if she is hospitalized, her congregation will help pay the bills, care for her children, and do the household chores until she recovers. The local church swings into action with meals and moral support after any sort of misfortune, from a catastrophic barn fire to a broken arm.

But with this security comes limitations—ones that seem stifling to non-Amish people accustomed to privacy and personal choice. Ask a convert who grew up in mainstream society to name the hardest thing about joining the Amish church, and he or she will quickly tell you that it wasn't giving up the car, putting on conspicuous clothing, logging off the Internet, or unplugging the Wii. It was having everyone know all about you and what you were doing every day. For the few dozen converts, many of whom were attracted to the Amish by the promise of a caring community, the reality can come as a shock.

A quick comparison of Amish and non-Amish church directories reveals strikingly different views of community. Non-Amish church directories typically include members' photos, street addresses, and e-mail addresses. Some list birthdays, but rarely birth years. In most churches you'd be considered rude if you asked someone's age, let alone published it for everyone to see. Age is considered a private matter.

In contrast, Amish church directories report year of birth as well as other personal and family information, including the names of parents and parents-in-law, marriage date, and often occupation. The directories list all of a married couple's children, regardless of age, as well as their birth dates, where each one lives, to whom they are married, and if they have joined the church. The directory does not include members' photos, which the Amish consider taboo, but that doesn't really matter, as everyone in the local congregation knows everyone else by sight. Amish directories provide detailed maps showing the location of each household. The content of these directories makes it clear: there are few secrets in this church.

"You Go First"

Think of our hero from the Western movie again. He's awfully good at getting rid of the bad guys, but it's harder to imagine him giving up his steed or his rifle if the town ever asked him to do so. His brand of heroism would vanish right along with his horse and his gun. But for real communities to function, each person must surrender at least some of his or her personal desires. Most people recognize this truth, but the Amish underscore it at every turn, convinced that life in community demands submission to God and others. "The first step to true brotherhood . . . [is] overcoming selfishness," Paul Kline, a retired business owner and deacon in Holmes County, Ohio, explains. "It is the utmost possible disappearance of everything personal and selfish."[3]

Unlike the modern quest to find one's self, Amish people seek to lose themselves. Personal ambition takes a backseat to scripture, church tradition, and family obligation. A common sign in Amish homes and schools proclaims that true JOY comes from putting *Jesus* first, *Others* next, and *Yourself* last.

Amish people often use the word *uffgevva*, which means "giving up," to describe surrendering selfish interests and desires. This self-surrender "often involves a battle of the wills," according to one Amish minister. It involves yielding one's personal will to God's will, submitting to the authority of others within the community (parents, teachers, church leaders), and submitting to the wisdom of the group.

The Amish see this attitude and habit of *uffgevva* exemplified by Jesus Christ, who willingly surrendered his life for the sake of others. "Christ was a king who lived and acted as a servant," explains Kline. "He submitted himself to God so completely that he never tried to do his own will by using his power to manipulate and force others." For Kline, "It is the church's intention and calling to give this principle bodily form by living it out in everyday life."

The way sermons are delivered also demonstrates the value the Amish place on submission. Amish ministers begin their sermons by confessing how unfit they feel to preach. And they conclude with a similar act of humility: asking the other ordained men present to correct any errors in their homilies. These customs, followed by ministers in every church service, signal that all members, including leaders, must submit themselves to some other authority.

The importance of submitting to others reveals itself in other ways as well. As worship concludes and members reassemble for a noon meal, they take their seats at tables in an order prescribed by gender, age, and seniority (in the case of leaders). The children watch and learn. Unlike many American children, they do not race to the front of the food line but wait patiently for their turn. Except for the very young, who are served fairly quickly, children eat after the adults have finished. The lesson of waiting has been ingrained in children long before they're teenagers, for training in *uffgevva* begins at an early age.

At occasions such as funerals, weddings, and community gatherings, where people's ages may not be known, men and women whisper, "You go first," "No, you," as they quietly defer to others. Even when traveling to church services, one mother noted, "It's an unspoken rule to never pass another buggy if you get behind a family with a slow horse. We are taught to be patient and not rush ahead of others."

The habits of humility mean that Amish people usually show reserve in their interactions with others. They often hesitate a moment before answering questions, resist posing for individual pictures, and decline to be quoted by name in newspaper stories lest they stand out or seem to be speaking for others. "In no way, whether in dress, behavior or attitude may a person raise himself above his fellows," Kline explains. "Only in this way is he able to be a part of a brotherhood."

Boxer Shorts or Briefs?

The Amish emphasis on *uffgevva* helps explain their practice of plain dress. Deacon Kline put it like this: "Most people in the world wear their clothes to enhance their reputation or to show off their bodies or to demonstrate their wealth." But doing this, he said, "is an expression of self-will" in which a person "tries to raise himself above his fellows. Our dress should show self-surrender." Of course, "every individual could decide his own standard of plainness, and some churches do this . . . [but] self-will must be yielded. . . . If it would be each individual's idea, then it would still be of the self."

Our explanation of *uffgevva* should not be carried too far. Although Amish society discourages individualism, it certainly does not extinguish all individual expression. Amish people have distinct likes and dislikes, personal preferences, and sometimes strong opinions. There is room aplenty for individual expression and creativity in the way a garden is planted, for example, or the colors and pattern chosen for a quilt. Hobbies such as woodworking or bird watching can be forms of individual expression. And competitive streaks often surface in a game of volleyball or ice hockey.

"The church doesn't tell us to wear boxer shorts or briefs, to go to McDonald's or Burger King," Jesse said. In fact, in his mind, "the idea that Amish give up all freedom of choice and let the community decide everything is a myth. Even if you do decide to let the church decide, that in itself is a choice."

But the message of self-denial is strong enough that ministers some-times need to remind members of their individual worth. "Just as the autumn landscape needs all the colors to complete [its] beauty," one preacher writes, characteristically drawing on an image from the natural world, "in the same way God needs all of us, every single one of us to make His plan complete. He needed someone just like you in His creation. That is why He made you looking like you do, and having the talents that you have."[4]

So although Amish people do not expect everyone in their com-munity to look, act, and think exactly alike, the range of individual expression is narrower than that of mainstream society. This communal orientation and these habits of submission shape their beliefs, practices, and affections—even their notion of salvation.

Born Again?

A few weeks after the story of Amish forgiveness at Nickel Mines circled the world, we had a call from a non-Amish friend. "Do you think the Amish are saved?" she asked. "Some members of my church think they aren't, and I want to know what you think."

Many religious traditions promise salvation—a way for individuals to be saved from the perilous conditions of this world and to attain life after death. From its beginning, Christianity has located salvation in the life, death, and resurrection of Jesus Christ. Today many Christians, especially evangelical Protestants, describe salvation as being "born again."

The term *born again* comes from a conversation reported in the New Testament's Gospel of John between Jesus and a Jewish religious leader named Nicodemus. Jesus told him, "Verily, I say unto thee, Except a man be born again, he cannot see the kingdom of God." A bit later, Jesus explained that "God so loved the world, that he gave his only begotten Son, that whosoever believeth in him should not perish, but have everlasting life" (John 3:3, 16).

Many Christians believe that these verses present the concept of salvation in a nutshell: those who believe that Jesus is God's son are "born again" and thus saved. Some Christians, in fact, pose the question, "Are you born again?" to determine the spiritual status of others. When Christian neighbors confront Amish people with that question, the Amish respond in bewilderment. "Of course," some say, "we teach the new birth all the time!" *

The Amish use of "new birth," *die Neugeburt*, in place of "born again" points to a distinctive understanding of Christian salvation.[5] In contrast to the individualistic connotation of being born again, the Amish view the new birth as a metaphor for joining a community—the church— much as natural birth brings a person into a biological family. The new birth can't take place in isolation. And given their awareness of nature, the Amish assume that birth implies pain and hard work. The "miracle of new birth takes place in nature all around us countless times every year," says one minister. "The small calf or the small colt gasps for its

---

*The entire new birth chapter of John's Gospel is read aloud in Amish church services twice each year as part of a five-Sunday sequence that culminates in communion, a significant ritual that we explore in Chapter Five.

first breath and thrashes around until it can stand on its own feet." Birth is "a struggle that is anything but easy."[6]

Some Christians who use the born again label also emphasize the assurance of salvation, the concept that those who confess their faith in Christ can be certain of their salvation right now, before God's final judgment. The Amish consider such a claim presumptuous. To them, salvation is a judgment that only God can make at the end of one's life. For that reason, they prefer to talk about a "living hope" rather than assurance of salvation. In the words of Eli, a midwestern Amish bishop, "We have a living hope. . . . We are in God's hands. We defer to God." For the Amish a living hope means a quiet confidence that in the end God will be a merciful and just judge.

Of course, references to a living hope also show that Amish people have confidence in their community's view of salvation. Although Amish are loath to judge the eternal destiny of others, some, such as Bishop Eli, are willing to explain their approach to salvation.

A One-Track Gospel

We sat in Eli's home one August evening, listening to the sounds of katydids outside his kitchen window. Obedience to the teachings of Jesus, he explained, is the reason why he rejects a "two-track system of salvation." By "two-track system" he means a theology that separates belief and obedience, placing personal faith on one track and matters of lifestyle on another. For Eli, salvation is personal but not private. He doesn't regard church-defined guidelines related to dress, technology, and leisure activities as optional add-ons. "I just don't like the two-track view of salvation that separates grace from ethics."

Even as Bishop Eli disapproves of a two-track approach to salvation, some non-Amish Christians criticize the Amish for trying to "earn" their salvation. These critics claim that the Amish way—mandating compliance with church teachings that ban electricity and owning cars, for example— distorts the notion that salvation is God's gift. Only God's free grace can save, the critics say, not obedience to the church's rules. The harshest critics think the Amish risk going to hell unless they embrace a different view of grace.

The Amish argue that such critics have a "narrow view of grace." Amish people see God's grace as "inseparably woven into the entire fabric of His relationship to His children—conviction, repentance, conversion, justification, a holy life, discipleship, yieldedness."[7] Another writer in the Amish magazine *Family Life* describes the Christian life as a stone arch holding up a bridge. Perhaps the "priceless verses in the third chapter of John . . . which tell us of the New Birth" are the keystone. But "we need the *complete* Gospel, not just a part. Start removing the stones in a bridge and the whole structure will soon crumble into a useless heap," he explains.

"There is much said today about accepting Christ as a personal Saviour," the writer continues. "Many even say that is absolutely all that you have to do to be sure that you are saved; nothing else. If we would follow such a gospel, we could live just about as we pleased. But salvation is not that cheap." Accepting "Christ as a Saviour from our sins" is necessary, he concludes, but it is just as necessary to "obey His commandments."[8] Although the Amish certainly see Jesus as their savior and friend, they are uncomfortable with a view of Jesus that overlooks obedience to his teachings.

The Amish view of salvation ultimately reaches back to the biblical understanding of the fear of God, a profound sense of respect for a transcendent and holy God. For them, reducing the Christian faith to just a "personal relationship with Jesus Christ" is inadequate in two ways: it shortchanges God's demand for holy living, and it discounts the importance of a Christian community to help individuals understand

and meet that demand. "In the multitude of counselors, there is safety," said Jesse, citing Proverbs 11:14.

Reading the Bible the Amish Way

This Amish accent on the community can also be seen in their approach to the Bible, which they consider to be God's word. They believe its contents are literally true, though they rarely use the terms *inerrancy* or *infallibility* to describe it.[9] Like many other Christians, Amish people read the Bible as part of their private and personal devotional lives. Many families have morning and evening devotions together, during which the father reads scripture and a prayer from *Christenpflicht* or another Amish prayer book.

But even though they use the Bible in devotional settings, they understand it to be primarily the church's book, a resource that—like every other part of life—cannot be properly or fully understood by a lone individual, or even by a small group of individuals apart from their local church. Thus schoolteachers read aloud from the Bible at the beginning of the school day, but Bible classes are not part of the school curriculum.

Even within the congregation, the Bible is an authority to be obeyed more than studied or analyzed. David Troyer, a noted nineteenth-century Amish bishop, epitomized this spiritual posture by concluding his religious essays with a paraphrase of Psalm 94:15: "Right must remain right, and to this all the upright in heart will submit."[10] At least one full chapter of the Bible is read aloud in each Amish worship service—much more than is read in most Protestant or Catholic church services—but members do not carry their Bibles to church on Sunday mornings.

Private devotional reading of scripture for personal inspiration is encouraged, but in-depth Bible study that might lead to individualistic interpretations is not. Those who show off their biblical knowledge or claim special revelation for their acts are seen as haughty and divisive because they turn the Bible on its head, using it as a tool for self-interest rather than as an authority to which individuals must surrender. Occasionally, some individuals study the Bible and declare a private revelation, such as "The Lord led *me* to start a new prison ministry program." "We are not to make the Bible suit our way of thinking," one minister warns.[11]

The Amish believe that the Lord guides a body of believers who diligently seek God's will together. And in Amish life that body is the local congregation. Amish skepticism of small-group Bible study arises because sometimes unhappy church members (or former members) use small-group Bible study to challenge church authority. "The Bible," said one Amish man, "is a mirror to examine ourselves, not a spotlight to shine on other people's shortcomings."

Letting Our Light Shine

Many Christians think of personal evangelism—witnessing to one's faith—as a verbal, one-on-one encounter. And although many believe it's important to urge new believers to join a church, others take the "lone ranger" route: ride into town, save a few souls, and move on.

Amish understandings of witness and mission could hardly differ more. Citing the words of Jesus, "Ye are the light of the world. A city that is set on a hill cannot be hid" (Matthew 5:14), they see their collective way of life as a public witness. In publications, sermons, and daily conversations, Amish people emphasize the importance of "letting our light shine," but as one man said, "not shining it in the eyes of other people."

"A Christian can be a good witness in many ways," notes an Amish writer in *Family Life*. "Living a good example has led more people to Christ than any amount of talking has ever done."[12] Another writer echoes this idea: "Plain clothes and a simple quiet life are certainly a Christian testimony which can have more far-reaching good influence on others than anything that we can ever say. A testimony does not necessarily mean for us to go up to a stranger and ask if he is saved."[13]

The concept of spreading the faith primarily through words strikes the Amish as hollow. They believe that the best way to judge a person's faith is to see it lived in context, in community. Unless they are asked, putting their faith into words for people they have never met before and may never see again makes little sense to them. There is little point, in their view, to inviting someone to a personal relationship with God without requiring obedience to a church-based lifestyle.

Ohio bishop David Troyer considered evangelism risky because the missionaries he observed did not follow church guidelines for daily conduct. He suspected that the unconverted would actually be better off without being exposed to such a faith, because Jesus had warned that "he who disregards one of the least commands, and teaches people so, will be rated least in the kingdom of heaven." In that case, Troyer concluded, "it will be more tolerable at God's judgment for the untaught heathen than for such who teach and are taught, and yet not correctly, especially for the ones who know better."

For Troyer and other Amish people, the problem with verbal evangelism is that it neglects the lengthy, formative process of submission and obedience in community. "My heart's wish is that all people of all manner and races and tongues might come to the Christian faith and be saved," Troyer emphasized. But verbal evangelism could simply not communicate the complete message of salvation.[14]

This doesn't mean that their collective Christian witness stays within their local zip codes. It's not uncommon for Amish groups to travel great distances to assist non-Amish people with cleanup following natural disasters, as many did following Hurricane Katrina. But Amish relief workers did not expect to convert others to the Amish way through such brief contact, even if their work was deeply appreciated. Their service was an end in itself, not an effort to proselytize. In fact, some Amish view the notion of seeking converts to one's own church as prideful. They hope that their Christian witness will lead others to deepen or renew their own faith rather than become Amish.

The worldwide media coverage of Amish forgiveness in the aftermath of the Nickel Mines schoolhouse shooting illustrates their style of witness. In the words of an Amish farmer, "Sometimes some of our people think we should do more evangelistic work or begin a prison ministry, but this forgiveness story made more of a witness for us all over the world than anything else we can ever do." "Maybe this was God's way to let us do some missionary work," another member said.

In Amish eyes, the effectiveness of their collective, public witness is confirmed by the millions of tourists who show an interest in their lives. In an essay titled "Learning from the Tourists," one Lancaster County Amish man notes, "Our ways of living may seem peculiar to an outsider, but we have deep joys that are totally unknown to the world. It behooves us all to be more content with the way of life handed down to us by our forefathers who denied themselves the pleasures of the world to be good examples to their descendants."[15]

So the Amish again bring us back to the core values of submission and community. These twin pillars uphold and secure the Amish way, which stands in stark contrast to other spiritual ways that grant greater priority to the individual. With its insistence that individuals submit to the community regardless of cost, the Amish way is deeply counter-cultural, perhaps even offensive to American sensibilities that consider individual privacy and personal freedom unassailable rights. Only a strong church community can make such a countercultural way of life possible or even thinkable. In the next chapter we venture further into the center of Amish church life and explore, among other things, how rules and standards are established.

CHAPTER FOUR

Joining Church

A person inside the church actually has more freedom, more
liberty, and more privilege than those outside.

—AMISH MINISTER

ave you seen this? Is this true?" asked our Amish friend Jesse.
He had sent us a newspaper column on a survey reporting
that about half of all Americans changed religious affiliation
during their lives, and that many people changed their religion or religious denomination more than once. The article included quotations
from "church hoppers," people who had switched churches looking for
a worship style that matched their tastes, or programs that better fit
their family's needs.[1]

Our friend was genuinely surprised. His Amish sensibilities led
him to expect the world to be faddish, so the concept of church hopping was not startling. He was taken aback, however, that a mainstream
newspaper columnist's critique would so closely mirror his own, that
she would suggest that Christians "should submit to the authority of a
church and not just walk away in the face of conflict."

Church hopping is hardly an option for Amish church members. For them, joining church is a lifelong commitment to God to participate with a particular group of people in a particular place. Those people and that place in Amish life is the *Gmay*—what other traditions call a local congregation or a parish.

People, Not Steeples

Driving through an Amish area, you won't see any Amish churches. That's because there aren't any. In fact, the Amish rarely use the German word *Kirche*, which suggests a church building. Instead, they use the Pennsylvania German word *Gmay*, a short form of *Gemeinde* or community, for both the local congregation and its worship services. Amish families gather for worship and fellowship in the homes of church members, underscoring their conviction that the church is a group of people, not a building or a meeting place.

The *Gmay* gathers every other Sunday morning, and households take turns hosting the services, which rotate around to all the homes with sufficient space. Members of the *Gmay* live within geographic boundaries known as the church district, often a square mile or two, but sometimes larger. For better or worse, a family's address determines its district, which means that changing churches isn't an option unless the family moves to a different district.

Each *Gmay* has its own set of leaders. Typically the bishop, the spiritual leader, performs the most important rituals, including baptisms, weddings, and funerals. The bishop is the only member who brings proposals for the congregation's consideration and action. Two ministers assist him, especially with preaching. The deacon helps the other leaders and coordinates material assistance for members with special financial needs.

A district typically includes twenty-five to forty households, usually 130 to 175 people. About 40 percent of them are baptized members, and the rest are children and unbaptized teenagers. When the number of people grows too large for them to gather in members' homes—as children are born or new families move into the area—the district divides and forms two new ones.

Thus congregations have a similar number of members. There are no Amish megachurches, and no communities of worship where some members know only a few others. Because members live near one another, the *Gmay* includes kin and close neighbors who often see one another throughout the week. This is the body to which Amish people commit themselves. Here they hold membership, and here they are held accountable for their conduct.

Certainly there is some mobility in Amish society. A family might move to a new settlement in another state, or a couple who began their married life on a rented farm may move to another district to buy land. In that sense, membership in the *Gmay* fluctuates, but church hopping as a matter of preference rarely occurs. Whether they move down the road or across the country, a family's new address dictates the *Gmay* in which they participate.

To Be or Not to Be?

Although Amish people have little choice regarding their church district, they do have a choice about church membership. The idea of voluntary church membership has a long history for the Amish, and it's one they take very seriously. As we saw in Chapter Two, some of their spiritual forebears, the Anabaptists, died for their convictions about adult baptism and church membership. Five hundred years later, the decision to join—or not to join—continues to be the most significant choice an Amish child will ever make. Although we've never met a parent who did not want his or her child to join the church, every parent knows that it's the child's choice and that some may reject the Amish way.

Before baptism, Amish children live under the discipline of their parents. They are not formally bound by the rules of the church because they are not yet members, though they follow established norms, such as wearing plain dress. Most parents grant their children more leeway after age sixteen, the time when teens begin to socialize with their peers and seek a spouse. This period of teenage "running around," often called *Rumspringa*, has attracted media attention because some teens rebel in dramatic ways—racing cars on rural roads or hosting beer parties, for example. For many youth, however, socializing during *Rumspringa* is more apt to involve hymn singing, volleyball games, and canoe trips. Even those who engage in activities the church discourages are generally doing things the rest of us would consider quite tame, such as waterskiing, snowmobiling, buying a cell phone, or going to a movie.

Rumspringa fascinates and perplexes outsiders, who wonder why seemingly sheltered children are allowed to "run wild" as teenagers. From an Amish perspective, *Rumspringa* looks quite different. First, no parents send their child into the world, either literally or figuratively. Teens continue to live at home, and those who engage in the most deviant behavior know that their parents strongly disapprove. *Rumspringa* also serves an important purpose in Amish theology: it underscores the belief that no one should be railroaded into church membership. Amish teens, meanwhile, are sorting out whether to accept the authority of the *Gmay* as they embark on adulthood. It's a weighty choice, and *Rumspringa* reminds them that they will be giving up a bundle of other choices should they opt for the church.

Eventually, about 90 percent of Amish teens choose baptism. The rest end up in a variety of spiritual camps: some in more liberal Anabaptist groups, some in evangelical or Pentecostal circles, and some in no church at all.

Baptized on Bended Knee

"I desire to have peace with God, and with the church. And I request that the church pray for me." These are the age-old sentences a young person speaks to the bishop when she or he decides to get baptized.[2] They are understated, humble words, but they carry a weight that non-Amish people can barely comprehend. Undertaken with eternity in mind, baptism proclaims that a person has chosen to submit to the *Gmay* for the rest of his or her life. "Baptism is an indication of our willingness to die to self [give up self-interests] . . . so that one can fit into the brotherhood as a useful member" is how Ohio deacon Paul Kline puts it.[3] Other life decisions usually hinge on the choice for church membership: whom to marry, where to live, and what kind of work to pursue. Few contemporary cultures contain a rite that so completely shapes how young people will live for the rest of their lives.

Baptisms usually take place in the spring or fall. Teens who plan to take that step tell their parents and their bishop, and the bishop announces it to the *Gmay*. On Sunday mornings during the months leading up to the baptism ceremony, the bishop and the ministers meet with the baptismal candidates for about thirty minutes during the beginning of the service while the rest of the congregation is singing. They gather in a separate room and review the Dordrecht Confession of Faith, known as the "Eighteen Articles," which summarizes core Amish beliefs.

Baptism takes place during a Sunday-morning worship service. At the close of a lengthy prayer, all the candidates kneel. The bishop then asks each one several questions:

"Can you *confess* . . . 'Yes, I believe that Jesus Christ is the Son of God'?

"Do you also recognize this to be a Christian order, church, and fellowship under which you now *submit* yourselves?

"Do you *renounce* the world, the devil with all his subtle ways, as well as your own flesh and blood, and desire to serve Jesus Christ alone, who died on the cross for you?

"Do you also *promise* before God and His church that you will support these teachings and regulations with the Lord's help, faithfully attend the services of the church and help to counsel and work in it, and not to forsake it, whether it leads you to life or to death?"[4]

After the candidates say yes to each question, the bishop cups his hands over the head of the first one, and a minister or deacon pours water into the bishop's hands. As the water trickles down over the applicant's head, the bishop says the person's name and "They that believe and are baptized shall be saved." He then pronounces the person baptized in the name of God the Father, Jesus Christ the Son, and the Holy Spirit. After all the baptisms have been completed, the bishop offers each candidate his hand, invites him or her to rise, and welcomes the new member into the church with a handshake and the "holy kiss of peace," a rite of fellowship mentioned in the New Testament. The bishop gives the kiss only to the men; his wife kisses the women.

After they've been baptized, the young adults enter into the life of the church in a new and fuller way. Their birthright community becomes their chosen community, one they cannot leave without severe consequences. Upon baptism, they are bound by the regulations of the church, and they have a voice and a vote in Members Meetings. They also have a role—though only a partial one—in selecting their ministers.

God's Search Committee

For young men, undergoing baptism entails another commitment: a promise to serve as bishop, minister, or deacon if chosen for such a position. There are no Amish seminaries or leadership training programs. Leaders come from the *Gmay*'s male membership and are selected by drawing lots, which minimizes human choice, and accents submission to God and the community. Our friend Reuben talked a bit about this divine drama in Chapter One.

The selection process begins when a leader dies, moves, or requests help due to age or chronic illness, or when a growing *Gmay* divides and the new district needs its own set of leaders. Ordinations typically take place at the end of a spring or fall communion service. Two weeks prior, the district's bishop or a visiting bishop preaches a sermon on the biblical qualifications for ministry. The bishop asks the church to pray for "men who are sound in the faith, preside well over their households, and have good order in their own homes."[5] These are the most important qualifications for ministry—not public speaking ability, administrative talent, or counseling skills. What matters is readiness to model the Amish way in daily habits, attitudes, and disposition.

The *Gmay* reassembles two Sundays later for a full day that reaches an emotional climax in late afternoon. After a period of silent prayer, the leaders go to a designated room in the house to receive nominations for the vacant position. One by one, each member—both male and female—files by the room and nominates a man for the role by

51

whispering his name to a leader. Most members offer one name, though some might not nominate anyone. No man nominates himself. In fact, anyone putting himself forward would certainly be disqualified as too proud.

After the nominations have been tallied, the bishop and other leaders return to the main room and announce the names of those with at least three nominations.* The tension in the room rises as the bishop asks the nominees to come forward—and there is no backing out when the church summons.

The bishop places identical hymnbooks, one per candidate, on a table in front of the nominees. One of the books, which have been shuffled in another room, contains a slip of paper that reads, "The lot is cast into the lap; but the whole disposing thereof is of the Lord" (Proverbs 16:33). Whoever chooses the hymnal containing the paper will be ordained. After a scripture reading, there is another long prayer, during which the entire *Gmay* kneels and silently pleads for God's intervention. Then everyone returns to her or his bench and the bishop says, "Now this is as far as humans can take it. The rest we let up to the Lord."

In breathtaking silence, each candidate selects a book. Then the bishop moves slowly from one man to the next, opening the hymnals and looking for the slip of paper to see on whom "the lot fell." When the bishop finds the paper, he asks the candidate to stand. Using words from a customary formula, the bishop ordains the new leader to a life-long position for which he received no formal training and will receive no salary.

"It's a weighty time," explained a man who had gone through the lot. "There are no congratulations. You realize that your life is now

---

*In some Amish groups, only two votes of nomination are required to place a person in the lot.

changed forever and you've now gotten an additional set of responsibilities that . . . you can only carry with the Lord's help."

Playing by the Rules

Americans sometimes speak of "nonpracticing" Catholics and "nonobservant" Jews, but such adjectives don't fit Amish life. To be Amish is to observe all things Amish: to practice the Amish way. Although leaders bear a special responsibility to uphold the rules and regulations of the church, the other members are expected to embrace them as well. Baptism obliges each member to submit to the *Gmay*'s regulations in matters large and small. "You are either in the church or you are outside; there is no happy medium," said one minister.[6]

The Amish use the German word *Ordnung* for the collective regulations, prohibitions, and expectations for an Amish lifestyle. *Ordnung* literally means "order," but the concept has broader connotations. It is the accumulated wisdom, the corporate guidelines that specify expectations for members.

The *Ordnung*, which members ratify twice a year, does not replace or supersede such obvious biblical commands as prohibitions against murder, adultery, and lying. Rather, the *Ordnung* seeks to apply biblical principles of humility, obedience, and nonresistance to everyday issues that the Bible doesn't directly address. Amish people do not equate the *Ordnung* with the Bible, but because the *Ordnung* is the church's application of scriptural principles, it's not optional. Members are expected to adhere to the guidelines as much as possible.

In this sense, the *Ordnung* is akin to the specific uniform worn by members of a sports team. No athlete believes that donning the uniform is the essence of the game or that it can substitute for skillful play. But wearing a uniform is required to play on the team, and wearing it certainly helps one's teammates win. If a team member asked to wear the opposing team's colors, the coach would certainly say no. In fact, simply asking such a question would show that the player misunderstands the game or else is not committed to the team. Of course, teams may modify their uniforms from time to time; but that's a team decision, not one that individual players can make on their own.

Every religious group has at least some expectations of its members. What is distinct about the Amish religious imagination is that it includes all of life, every day. To continue the sports team analogy: for the Amish, the game is never over, and all the rules matter. It's never time to leave the field or take off the uniform. Sunday-morning church attendance is a religious practice, but so too are Thursday-afternoon decisions about using electricity or driving a car. From this perspective, it makes perfect sense to the Amish that the *Ordnung* would spell out mundane matters such as the dimensions of a bonnet or the length of a beard.

The *Ordnung* is not identical across Amish communities or even from one *Gmay* to the next in the same geographical area. The *Ordnung* in one community may dictate gray buggies, whereas those in other communities may mandate black or white ones. Some *Gmays* permit businesses to use hydraulic power, while others, just a few miles down the road, do not. Because the *Ordnung* is rooted in church tradition, it respects and preserves local custom and tends to resist innovation.

The *Ordnung* can be highly detailed, as in the rules governing buggies in one southern Indiana community: "Buggies can be made with plywood and covered with black vinyl. Doors can be snap or slide, for single-seated buggies a door on each side and on back, for two seated buggies two sets of doors on side and/or on back, plain rearview mirror for safety, head lights and tail lights on one or both sides. Triangle and reflector tape, not for luxury, but for safety." There are instructions, too, for newly baptized members who must adapt their buggies to meet church standards: "On tops already made, all window frames must be painted black, lining must be black. All colored lining must be changed. . . . Tape players, radios, CBs, etc. must be removed. No tinted windows."[7]

This example is unusual only because it was written down. The *Ordnung* typically takes the form of oral tradition, communicated through lived example. Amish people know the *Ordnung*—it's not ambiguous—but most would be hard-pressed to recite all its dos and don'ts. Because the *Ordnung* deals with the details of daily life, it is "caught" more than it is taught. It is simply absorbed in the course of everyday life. Thus mothers and fathers play a much larger role in transmitting the *Ordnung* than do bishops and ministers.

One mother uses the analogy of typing to explain the role of parents in cultivating obedience to the *Ordnung*. "When I was learning to touch type, it soon became apparent that the key to success was to repeat and to keep on repeating the exercises," she explains. "Over and over and over, the same words, the same keys, the same combinations of letters," all became habitual. "Thus the fingers learn to fly to the right keys without any conscious thought. Such repetition 'planted' something into the fingers, a skill that would remain for life."[8] In the same way, daily household routines instill in children the virtues of the *Ordnung* without relying on lectures, sermons, or written lists of rules.

Holding the Line

The *Ordnung* changes slowly, usually after lengthy discussion, discernment, and the endorsement of members, both men and women. The bishop plays an important role in these changes, working to maintain consensus and deal with dissent. But because his authority is also governed by the *Ordnung*, he cannot simply dictate rules. "This did not come on overnight," a Pennsylvania minister emphasizes when explaining how the *Ordnung* functions, "nor did it come through rash or harsh commands of our bishops. . . . The bishops and ministers do not make the *Ordnung*, nor do they draw the line; they only attempt to hold the line."[9]

"Holding the line" reveals a good deal about Amish spirituality. Theologically, the *Ordnung* is rooted in a belief that God created an orderly natural world and that human life is best lived in harmony with and in submission to God's will. To discern this sort of orderly life, the Amish rely on scripture and tradition as wise guides. Noted Amish minister Joseph F. Beiler points to Jesus' parable of the wise man who built his house on rock (Matthew 7:24–27) to explain the purpose of the *Ordnung*. The house on a solid foundation survived the storms, Jesus said, while the one built on sand collapsed. Both houses initially looked alike, but time proved otherwise.

For Beiler, history reveals which foundations the church can trust, and he cautions against carelessly discarding proven tradition. "Over the centuries this [Amish] house of God has stood the storms of persecution," he points out. Other denominations "use the same Bible faithfully; they have hymnbooks, creeds, the best devotional materials ever available at any time since the beginning," but many have not endured. "There must be another element that played a role in the house that stands," Beiler concludes. He believes that this missing element was a patient respect for tradition, one that refused to grant new ideas superiority over those of the past.

Beiler's perspective clarifies how the *Ordnung* relates to the Bible. The Amish do not claim that every—or even most—church regulations can be supported by a specific verse from scripture. They do maintain, however, that each guideline is based on a biblical principle. Thus the *Ordnung* is considered a cluster of time-tested practices that enhance community well-being. And compliance with it signals a member's desire to live in harmony with others. "Since obedience is a close associate to *Ordnung*," Beiler explains, "it is a symbol that tells if you care for church or if you don't care, if you love the church or if you don't." Repeatedly snubbing the *Ordnung* is seen as sin, not because its regulations are on par with the Ten Commandments, but because flouting it reveals a spirit of arrogance and self-centeredness. Living by the community's collective blueprint indicates a patient and humble heart. A church formed by the habits of the *Ordnung*, Beiler concludes, "generates peace, love, contentment, equality and unity."

Any Place for Grace?

Few outsiders see virtue or value in the *Ordnung*. Many Americans conclude that it's oppressive, because it denies basic rights of self-determination and personal expression. Who would give up the freedom to dress as they like and pursue the profession of their choice? Who would surrender such decisions to tradition or the discernment of a group?

Some Christians dismiss such rules as sheer legalism. They see the Amish way as a life of grim determination, a graceless exercise in gritting one's teeth and trying to do the right thing. For these outsiders, following the *Ordnung* demonstrates not faithfulness to Jesus Christ but a futile effort to secure God's favor. "Enforcing man-made rules in your home is acceptable," writes one ex-Amish member, "but when you start doing the same in a church it becomes religious legalism [that] subverts and diminishes God's grace."[10]

Jesse noted, however, that "accepting God's grace doesn't mean you can just do as you please." Most Amish people know that the concept of the *Ordnung* makes little sense to outsiders. "It is only a person who has learned to love . . . a respected church *Ordnung* who can ever

57

fully appreciate its values," Beiler concedes. "It gives freedom of heart, peace of mind and a clear conscience."[11]

The Amish agree that their approach to faith, like any other one, has its share of potential pitfalls. To their credit, they generally interpret the *Ordnung* with generous flexibility for people with special needs, such as those with health issues or physical challenges.* And they are quick to admit that the *Ordnung* can be "overenforced" and thus severed from its spiritual roots. One Amish author warns that "without an inner change of heart," doing the right things is hypocrisy, merely a "show of holy living . . . so that people will look upon us as good people."[12] Preacher Beiler agrees: "Church *Ordnung* cannot be lived by the letter alone. It must be lived in Spirit."[13]

Nurturing that spirit—the spiritual roots of the community and of the members who commit themselves to it—is not left to happenstance. A deliberate rhythm of worship, along with annual rituals of confession and renewal, foster Amish faith and faithfulness. To these rhythms and rituals we now turn.

---

*Examples of flexibility include the use of battery-powered wheelchairs and the use of electrical generators for special medical equipment in the home.

CHAPTER FIVE

Worshiping God

I don't think anything compares to the sacredness
and holiness of our communion service.

—AMISH MOTHER

The room is remarkably quiet, considering that more than
two hundred people are sitting in a modest-size basement.
We feel crowded, packed tightly onto the backless benches
with our knees almost touching the bench in front of us. Later
we overhear Amish people saying how open and roomy this space
felt. It's clear to us once again that, among the Amish, *we're* the
peculiar ones.

Around 9:00 A.M., without a word of welcome, a middle-aged
man calls out a hymn number from his seat, just loud enough for others
to hear. Picking up hymnals that had been scattered along the benches,
everyone finds the page in the small, black book with *Ausbund* on the
spine. The man who announces the hymn is the song leader, but he
does not stand in front of the congregation, keep time, or in any way

perform. In fact, he sits in the midst of the congregation and simply begins to sing.*

The hymn is familiar to everyone—just as familiar as it was to their great-great-grandparents. We listen as the song leader's voice rises and falls as he slowly draws out the notes for the first syllable. Then the rest of the congregation joins in.

A Twenty-Minute Hymn

To modern ears, Amish singing seems agonizingly slow. The Amish sing in unison, in German, in a style that professional musicians call melismatic and that outsiders often say sounds like Gregorian chant or Torah chanting. The congregation draws out each syllable, sliding between notes for each one. Because the *Ausbund* contains only words and no music, the melodies pass orally through the generations.[1] "The singing in unison is . . . a form of oneness and a blending together," says Amish deacon Paul Kline.[2]

The ethos of the worship service embodies what the Amish call *Gelassenheit*, a word that suggests a profound acceptance of God's providence and timing. This sense of resignation to God's will means letting go of things, giving up control, and not striving against the circumstances of life. Outward expressions of humility, patience, and a quiet spirit show that members have yielded themselves to God and to each other. The spirit of *Gelassenheit* brings a sense of contentment and harmony as members worship together.

When the first hymn ends, the song leader doesn't have to choose the next one, because the second hymn in an Amish service is always the

---

*Several men in the congregation serve as song leaders. If visitors from other *Gmays* are present, they are often asked to lead a song.

same. This song, known as the *Loblied* (praise hymn), has four stanzas asking God to bless the preachers and make the worshipers receptive to God's message. In translation the second and third verses include these words:

> Open the mouth of Thy servants, Lord,
> And give them wisdom also,
> That they may rightly speak Thy Word
> Which encourages a devout life.
>
> . . . .
>
> That we may become acquainted with Thy Word,
> And thus become devout
> And live in righteousness,
> Taking heed to Thy Word always,
> And thus remain undeceived.[3]

Depending on local tradition, it may take eighteen to twenty-five minutes to sing the *Loblied*'s four verses. No one is hurried. Even time, bending to the spirit of *Gelassenheit*, is yielded rather than forced.

Worship reflects and reinforces Amish beliefs, and perhaps more than any other community practice, it shapes their affections for God. Although their spirituality is woven into everyday life in various ways, the Amish place a high value on Sunday worship. Each *Gmay* gathers every other Sunday, and all members are expected to attend.* A serious illness would be the only excuse for staying home. On the Sundays when their church does not meet (the "off-Sundays"), families have more flexibility.

---

*Holding church services every other Sunday is an old tradition (also common among non-Amish rural churches in the 1800s) that likely developed because horse-drawn travel was difficult on rural roads for much of the year, and to accommodate the role of the family in religious education on the off-Sunday.

Typically they stay at home and have family devotions. Occasionally they attend the worship services of a neighboring district, adding visitors to most services.

Folks Are a-Coming

Getting a house ready to host more than two hundred guests is no small feat. For the family hosting *Gmay*, preparation begins a month in advance with yard work, housecleaning, preparing food, moving furniture, and arranging benches to accommodate all the guests. Depending on the community, the layout of the house, and the season of the year, the family may arrange to have *Gmay* on the first floor of their home, in their basement, or in their barn or shop. Each district has a "church wagon" or "bench wagon" to transport their benches and hymnbooks from one home to another. The bench wagon may also carry boxes of plates, cups, and eating utensils for the noon meal following the service.

Rotating *Gmay* from one home to another means that the families in a district will visit each other's homes about once a year, reinforcing the sense of intimacy within the community. Families look forward to hosting worship. At the same time, getting ready takes a good deal of work, as one teenage girl suggests in this poem she wrote about Saturday cleaning and last-minute preparations.

> Hustling, bustling, running about,
> Around the house, in and out.
> Wash the woodwork, the windows, the walls,
> Sweep the boys' room and the hall.
>
> Fix the water, get the mop by the pump.
> It'll all be done in a hop, skip, and jump.

Now that the cleaning has all come to a stop
We are generously treated with ice cream and pop!

We eat the breakfast as fast as we can,
Then wash the dishes and put away the pans.
The folks are a-coming, they're right on the spot,
For church will start at 9 o'clock![4]

The first buggies arrive early, as close family members come to help with final preparations. Other members begin showing up around 8:00 A.M., and as buggies unload, families slip apart, reconfiguring the *Gmay* by age and gender. Older women gather in one part of the house, young mothers and babies in another, and teenage girls in yet another. The men stand in the barnyard, while the boys act as hostlers, or caretakers of the horses, unhitching them and taking them to the barn for food and water. Young boys follow their fathers and young girls their mothers.

Assembling for worship follows a prescribed routine. The home bishop walks in first, followed by any visiting bishops and ministers, in an order determined by the length of their ordination. After them come the home ministers, followed by the deacon. Next the married men file in by age, down to the youngest one. Meanwhile, the women are also entering through another door, again from oldest to youngest. Each group moves toward its traditional seating area: older men in one section, older women in another, and so on. Young children sit with one of their parents or grandparents. The oldest people may be given folding chairs, but everyone else will spend the next three hours on backless benches.

The teenage boys often enter last, and as nine o'clock approaches, the household host goes outside to tell them it's time to come in. Sam Stoltzfus, an Amish grandfather, remembers what it was like in his boyhood *Gmay* as he and his friends prepared to enter the service. "We would brush off our trousers, and the big boys would comb their hair," he recalls, and then they would slowly walk in. "All the boys would always pass the ministers, shake their hands, and then sit down just behind the ministers on three or four long benches. In our district there were approximately forty-five boys, so this took about five minutes."[5]

In the meantime everyone has been waiting quietly. Finally the song leader begins the first hymn. "Our seating arrangement and how we go in according to age all is a form of *Gelassenheit*," Paul Kline explains. "Each one has his place, no one needs to assert himself."[6] The entrance and seating patterns, determined by age, gender, and rank of office, are similar in all churches, but the specific arrangements vary somewhat depending on the location of the service.

Patient Worship

As soon as the singing begins, the ordained leaders get up and leave in the same order they entered. They confer in another room, where they begin with a silent prayer. After the prayer, the group decides who will preach the two sermons of the morning. Each leader comes to church knowing that he might be asked to preach, but no one prepares sermon notes in advance. Agreeing at the last minute to preach a lengthy sermon is yet another act of submission, of giving up control.

Sometime during the singing of the *Loblied*, the leaders return to the worship service and resume their places on a bench among the congregation. When the *Loblied* concludes, a preacher rises to deliver the opening sermon, which may last a half hour. Symbolic of his servant status and equality with other members, the preacher stands on the open floor without podium or pulpit.

Like all spoken but unread parts of the service, the opening sermon is delivered in the Pennsylvania German dialect (except in a few districts that use a Swiss dialect). The message reminds the congregation why it has gathered and calls all members to humble themselves before God. "My uncle Jonas often mentions the story of Simeon in the Temple, when Simeon blessed [baby] Jesus," Reuben, a minister, told us. The Bible says that "the Holy Spirit brought Simeon to the temple that day, and we should be coming to our church the same way: brought by the Holy Spirit, not just by habit." Attuned to the rhythms of the seasons, the opening sermon often mentions the weather or the beauty of creation and God's role as creator and provider. As the sermon concludes, everyone kneels for a silent prayer.

Following the prayer, everyone rises and stands for the reading of scripture, usually one full chapter, read from Martin Luther's German translation. The particular Bible passage that is read is determined by the lectionary, the yearlong calendar of biblical texts used in worship (see Appendix II). "If this pattern were not followed, then the tempta-tion would be to just preach on the pet doctrines of the ministers," Deacon Kline explains.[7]

Many Christian communities use lectionaries, though the texts vary somewhat from one tradition to another. The Amish lectionary readings are *entirely* from the New Testament. About two-thirds of them are from the Gospels—the books of the Bible that recount the life, teaching, miracles, death, and resurrection of Jesus Christ—and most are from the Gospel of Matthew.

"We are very much focused on Jesus Christ as the son of God, and so the words and teaching and works of Jesus are very important," noted Reuben. Another minister underscores the significance of Jesus' Sermon on the Mount, found in Matthew 5–7. "In it, Jesus gave His listeners that masterpiece on the 'how' of living a Christian life," the minister emphasized. The sermon covers "almost any situation that

65

could come up in anybody's life" and "is just as much for us today as it was for His listeners nearly two thousand years ago."[8] Although some Christians regard Jesus' Sermon on the Mount as an impractical ideal, the Amish think it should be followed literally.

I Don't Know Where I'm Going

Non-Amish Christians who are used to lively sermons enhanced with video clips or PowerPoint slides might be surprised at—or put to sleep by—the quiet cadence of an Amish sermon. The hour-long main sermon, which follows the Bible reading, embodies the values of humility and submission. Preachers typically begin with a biblical blessing, such as "Grace be unto you, and peace, from God our Father, and from the Lord Jesus Christ" (1 Corinthians 1:3), and then confess their unworthiness to preach.

"One of the basic ideas you try to get across," Reuben told us, "is 'Here I am, I don't know where I'm going [with the sermon], please pray for me.' . . . One thing I also say is, 'I don't need to tell you my weaknesses because you can easily see them.'" Even seasoned preachers privately express their continuing need for humility and *uffgevva* as they give themselves up to God, without any sermon notes, for an hour.

Although bishops and ministers have no seminary training, they are prepared in other ways. Most sermons are patterned on a style of preaching that they have heard since they were children. Given the system of choosing ministers by drawing lots, every man knows he is a potential candidate. And that prospect prods men and boys to pay attention in church. "You never know if you might be the next preacher!" Reuben explained. "So you watch and listen and get ideas."

In addition, bishops and ministers know the lectionary calendar, and they read the scheduled texts several times before each Sunday service. The main sermon always uses the week's scripture reading as a starting point, but then often draws on Old Testament stories, the Psalms, and illustrations from contemporary life.

Some of the preparations Reuben makes as he anticipates preaching include reading the scripture text in German, looking in *Büchner's German Concordance* for other biblical passages related to the theme, and getting outside ideas from the *Life Application Study Bible* or other books, such as *Happenings of the Bible* and *The Day Christ Died*. Despite such preparation, "You never know what will come forth [when preaching]," Reuben confessed. "You make mental notes as you study the text. . . . But when you sit down later [after the sermon], sometimes you are surprised by what you said, and you credit that to the work of the Holy Spirit."

Following the main sermon, several of the ordained men offer *Zeugniss* (testimony). They comment on the sermon and correct any errors the preacher may have made. "Sermons are subject to *Zeugniss* in order to ensure that . . . one man cannot run away with his pet theories," Deacon Kline explains.[9] This rite underscores a remarkable fact: no one, not even the bishop, has the final word within the *Gmay*. Everyone must submit to someone and, in a way, to everyone.

After *Zeugniss* the congregation again kneels while one of the ministers reads a prayer from *Christenpflicht*, which ends with the Lord's Prayer. The service concludes with a benediction and a final *Ausbund* hymn sung in a slow cadence.

It is not surprising that patience is a common theme in the worship service. In fact, one mother pointed out that seven of the lectionary readings emphasize patience and related ideas such as endurance or steadfastness, which "mean the same thing as patience," in her words. And Jesse noted that, although it's not in the lectionary, Colossians 3:12–13 is frequently mentioned by ministers. He quoted the passage from the New International Version: "Therefore as God's chosen people holy and dearly loved, clothe yourselves with compassion, kindness, humility, gentleness and patience. Bear with each other and forgive whatever grievances you may have against one another. Forgive as the Lord forgave you." For Jesse, these verses are a key to understanding Amish spirituality.

Following the service, the men transform the worship space once again, rearranging the benches and setting up tables for the noon meal prepared by the women of the host household. Although everyone shares in the meal, there is not space for everyone to sit at once, so people eat in shifts with others of their age and gender. The simple meal (soup or sandwiches; pickles, beets, cheese, or other side dishes; pie; coffee) follows a traditional menu determined by the community. Having a set menu reduces the host family's work and eliminates any competitive impulse to outdo another's meal. Everyone lingers into the afternoon, visiting with one other. Relatives may stay longer to help with cleanup. In many communities, the young people return to the host home in the evening for socializing and singing German and English hymns and gospel songs.

The Amish style of worship may seem strange to people accustomed to more spontaneity. The somber faces, serious sermons, and slow singing may lead some people to conclude that Amish worship is a dry, tradition-bound ritual. Of course, all religious communities have traditions, even those with a less restrained and more lively style of worship. Amish or not, spontaneous or not, religious practices create patterns that, week in and week out, year after year, shape religious affections in certain ways. For the Amish, worship is a reminder that God is best adored by patient waiting and yielding to one another in time-tested ways. These ways may puzzle those unable to sit patiently through a three-hour service, but for the Amish they offer quiet peace in a perilous world.

Preparing for the Lord's Supper

The Amish do not observe Advent, Lent, or other historic seasons of the church year, but they do have a distinct ritual calendar that underscores the value of submission and the importance of unity in the *Gmay*. The highest and holiest moment of the Amish church calendar is the communion service, which is held twice a year, once near Easter and again in October.* Patterned after Jesus' last meal with his disciples, communion commemorates his death through the sharing of bread and wine.

It is hard to exaggerate the importance of communion in Amish life. Unlike most Protestant and Catholic observances of communion, which focus on an individual's standing before God, the Amish observance includes a communal dimension. For them, communion celebrates the unity of the *Gmay* as the people of God. For this reason, communion requires a time of preparation stretching over five Sundays, a prelude that stresses forgiveness and harmony within the church. And unlike communion in the larger Protestant and Catholic world, among the Amish, if discord prevails, the Lord's Supper may be postponed for weeks or even months.

The five-Sunday sequence begins with the so-called New Birth Sunday, followed by an off-Sunday, Council Meeting, another off-Sunday, and finally Holy Communion. On New Birth Sunday the lectionary texts include John 3, and the main sermon focuses on the story of Jesus and Nicodemus and the necessity of the new birth. Baptisms are scheduled for this Sunday if there are candidates.

---

*Holding communion twice a year has been a tradition since the Amish began in 1693. The five-Sunday sequence of preparation discourages a more frequent observance.

Two weeks after New Birth Sunday, the *Gmay* gathers for Council Meeting. This Sunday-morning service accents mutual submission and an affirmation of the *Ordnung*. In the first part of the service, a minister recounts the creation story in Genesis, the flood, the patriarchs, Old Testament prophecies of a promised savior, and then the birth, ministry, crucifixion, and resurrection of Jesus.

In Matthew 18, the cornerstone scripture for the day, Jesus tells his disciples that, to enter the kingdom of heaven, they must humble themselves and become like small children. He also instructs them to reconcile disagreements and forgive one another, dozens of times if needed. Hence ministers admonish members to forgive those who have wronged them, so that the *Gmay* can celebrate the Lord's Supper in unity two weeks later. "Forgiveness is always the theme of Council Meeting," a bishop explained. "If anyone has an unforgiving attitude, they can't partake in communion." The message is clear: purge any grudges and repair broken relationships so that all can participate with clean hearts.

The second part of Council Meeting (for members only) is the *Abstellung*, which means to "put away" or place off-limits. The bishop cites 1 Corinthians 14:33 and 40, "For God is not the author of confusion, but of peace" and "Let all things be done decently and in order." Then he outlines the *Ordnung*, reminding everyone of the *Gmay*'s commitment to simplicity and humility. Typically, the bishop begins by reviewing expectations for men's clothing, hairstyles, and so on. Expectations for women come next, including an emphasis on mothers' responsibility to nurture moral values in their children. Then he recounts prohibitions on such things as certain technologies and playing competitive sports in organized public leagues. The *Abstellung* concludes with admonitions against sexual immorality, alcohol abuse, drug use, and greed. "These should not have to be mentioned with God's people,"

one elderly bishop said, "but it seems warnings about these are necessary, given human nature."

At the conclusion of the service, the ministers ask each member if
he or she is ready for communion. "This is a time of proving ourselves,
and asking whether the vows made at baptism are still being kept," said
Reuben. "Only when we are in unity with the *Ordnung* and with one
another can [communion] be observed." First each ordained leader says,
from his seat, "If communion can be held, I wish to participate, in my
weakness. If I could be accepted, it would bring me deep joy. If I have
offended anyone with words or deeds, I wish to be admonished about
it in love, and would also hope to receive it in the same way, and make
things right, with the Lord's help."[10] Then each member responds with
similar words.

Council Meeting is not a mere formality. If a cluster of members
is not ready, not in harmony with each other or the *Ordnung*, communion may stall for weeks or months until the disagreement or dispute
is resolved. Communion might be postponed, for example, if the
congregation is at an impasse over the best way to deal with a member
with an addiction, to change a technological practice, or to discipline
a wayward minister. If only one or two members are quarreling or
disgruntled with the church, communion will proceed without them,
but the goal is full harmony. Council Meetings encourage deep soul-
searching as members ponder their duty to forgive and to purge their
hearts of bitterness. They are urged to confess their sins and to give
themselves up completely to God and the *Gmay* so that all can celebrate
unity in the upcoming communion service.

On the off-Sunday that follows Council Meeting, members in
some communities fast in the morning and spend time in introspection
and prayer. A prayer for this day in the *Lust Gärtlein* devotional book
includes a lengthy series of confessions and asks God's help to "put off

71

all envy, hate, and vengefulness of heart, and love and forgive everyone, as Thou also have loved me and forgiven me in Christ."[11]

The Amish take very seriously the apostle Paul's warning against those who "eateth and drinketh unworthily" (1 Corinthians 11:29)—those who participate in communion without first mending ruptured relationships. Thus members may seek out one another during communion season to heal old wounds in their relationships. Both at Council Meeting and again just prior to communion, each member affirms that he or she is at peace with others and ready to proceed with the holy event. On both days, the response needs to be unanimous, or nearly so, for the service to proceed.

The Holiest Days of the Year

Communion Sunday, the twice-yearly high point of the Amish year, is a lengthy service that stretches from about 8:00 A.M. to 4:00 P.M. without a formal break. During the lunch hour, people quietly take turns eating in small clusters in an adjoining room.

After the singing but before the first sermon, members reiterate their commitment to unity and desire for communion. Following the bishop's lead, each minister and then each member affirms his or her peace with God and the *Gmay*.

The sermons that day follow a prescribed pattern. They survey a large portion of biblical history, beginning with creation and continuing through an overview of the Acts of the Apostles. The first preacher tracks the Israelites' exodus from Egypt, the Jewish Passover feast, and God's command to observe it yearly as a reminder of his saving power. This preacher shifts back and forth between the patriarchs and Jesus, explaining, for example, that Jesus kept the Passover with his disciples but "gave His flesh and blood to redeem mankind from sin . . .

and [then] commanded that his apostles and later, his church, should observe this feast in remembrance of Him."[12]

The second sermon summarizes Jesus' life, death, and resurrection. Jesus' submission to God, his self-giving love for others, and his suffering in the face of evil are held up as models for daily living. The sermon concludes with a reading of one of the Gospel accounts of the Last Supper, in which Jesus washes the feet of his disciples, and a communion prayer from *Christenpflicht*.

Now well into the afternoon, the bishop thanks the congregation for its expression of unity, and he "gives the glory and honor to the Lord for the privilege to be together in such circumstances." He then breaks pieces of bread from a loaf and offers them to members as a symbol of Jesus' body broken on the cross. After this, the congregation drinks wine from a single cup to commemorate the blood of Jesus Christ.

When speaking of the bread and wine, the bishop stresses that each member is like a grain of wheat that is crushed to produce a loaf of bread, and like a grape that is pressed to make a bottle of wine. One bishop explained, "If one grain remains unbroken and whole, it can have no part in the whole . . . if one single berry remains whole, it has no share in the whole . . . and no fellowship with the rest." These metaphors encourage individuals to yield their wills for the welfare of the larger body.

One final act remains in the daylong drama. Patterned after the example of Jesus, who washed his disciples' feet in an act of humble service (John 13:1–20), church members divide into pairs—men with men, women with women—and remove their shoes and socks. Bending over a basin of warm water, each washes his or her partner's feet and dries them with a towel. The two then stand and conclude with a handshake and a holy kiss. In the words of the Dordrecht Confession, this rite is "a sign of true humility and lowliness" that also symbolizes "the true washing, when we are washed through His precious blood and purified in our souls."[13]

Footwashing does something else, too. As a physical and menial task, this bodily ritual concludes the holiest days of the Amish year with a stark reminder of the very practical and sometimes unpleasant realities of community. Having affirmed the importance of that community throughout the long communion season, members know that their life together remains imperfect, prone to petty problems and conflicts. Sustaining the joy of unity over the next six months will require ongoing effort and all the patient virtues that their worship has nourished.

CHAPTER SIX

Living Together

Discipline is important anywhere people are to live together
in peace, and especially so in the church.

—AMISH LEADER[1]

When doctors told the Amish parents that their babies would survive, the couple's relief and joy were immeasurable. Their premature twins had arrived with a host of complications, but the Indiana couple decided to accept the advanced technology necessary to keep them alive. Shortly after the twins came home, the family received a hospital bill that nearly topped a million dollars.

Such a bill would shake most Americans. For those without insurance, it would be a prescription for bankruptcy. Even for those with insurance, copayments, lifetime-benefit limits, premium increases, or a policy cancellation could jeopardize their financial futures.

Most Amish are troubled by rising health care costs, too, but their options and responses are decidedly different. With a few exceptions Amish people do not carry commercial insurance, nor do they participate in Medicare, Medicaid, or Social Security.* Although individual households cover their own medical bills as they are able, they often rely on the support of their *Gmay* or other Amish congregations in their region, especially for large expenses.[2] Many Amish communities have negotiated discounts with local hospitals if they pay in cash within thirty or sixty days. Rounding up that cash is no small undertaking, but in nearly every case the church comes through—as it did for the new parents in Indiana.

Whereas health care evokes everything from awe to outrage among American consumers, for the Amish it's an arena for spiritual formation and definition—from the act of declaring their church membership to qualify for a hospital's cash-payment discount to helping one another so that their community can thrive. In a financially perilous world, mutual aid—the assistance that church members know they can count on—not only offers a crucial safety net but also articulates the deepest bonds of care within the *Gmay*.

Mutual Care Instead of Insurance

Many American Christians would say that they are part of a caring church that supports them in many ways, but few rely solely on their church to cover their medical costs. The courage to reject commercial insurance and government aid in modern society is only possible with the enduring help of a community of faith to assist with major medical expenses. The Amish believe that commercial insurance is "an attempt to make secure that which Jesus said is not secure." True security for them comes when members take care of one another as

---

*Although the Amish do not pay Social Security taxes, they do pay income (federal, state, local), sales, inheritance, and property taxes.

much as possible. One Amish guidebook says that in "the world's system of insurance . . . the poor man's premiums are included in replacing the rich man's loss. In the Scriptural pattern, the situation is reversed. . . . There are no selfish motives involved."[3]

During the 1950s and 1960s, Amish people stoutly resisted participation in the U.S. Social Security program, insisting that it was the responsibility of families and churches to care for their own elderly and orphans. The Amish won exemption in 1965 largely because of their decades-long record of mutual care. The widespread use of *Dawdyhauses* (grandparent houses), built for in-laws and usually attached to family dwellings, testifies to this practice.

Amish charity has increasingly shifted from helping with fire and storm damage to covering the medical bills of members. Although procedures vary from one community to another, deacons always oversee the process. Each *Gmay* collects alms twice a year around communion time, when households donate to the deacon fund for community needs. Deacons have discretion in distributing the money, often to widows, the ill, and families with unusual bills.[4]

Communities meet the costs of larger and unexpected needs in various ways. Some have fire and storm aid plans, in which church members pay assessments and trustees make disbursements. Fund-raising efforts such as benefit suppers and charity auctions are common ways to defray mounting medical bills. In a festival-like atmosphere, auction-goers bring goods to sell, and auctioneers donate their skills to sell the items—in some cases back to the very people who brought them! These events, filled with fun and fellowship, are successful community efforts to aid the needy.

This does not mean that individual families bear no financial responsibility. "Charity should begin at home," writes one Amish leader. "If someone has a loss or hospital bill, he should pay what he can himself. Beyond that, his relatives are responsible to help." This leader admits, however, that some costs require the help of the local congregation and "sister congregations" when the need is large. "If the people have the right love for each other and are willing to share the blessings God has given them, such a plan will work."[5]

A Thinking-of-You Shower

Amish mutual aid occurs in more ordinary ways as well. The most legendary, visible form of mutual aid is the barn raising, when neighbors gather to rebuild a fire-ravaged barn, but because many Amish people now work in small shops, on constructions crews, and in other nonfarm jobs, fewer barns need replacing. Still, all Amish families receive practical aid from their community when they need a helping hand.

For example, a mother with five small children said, "If I need to go to town and need a babysitter, I have three cousins living within a mile of here, where I can drop off some of my girls anytime." Following childbirth, whether at home or in a clinic or hospital, grandmothers, mothers, aunts, or sisters come to stay with the mother for a week or more, helping with the new baby and caring for other children. Neighbors may bring meals for even longer. And if a person is injured, church members assist with household and farm chores. One farmer in Ohio explained how he and a half dozen other Amish neighbors spent two days plowing the fields of a church member who was hospitalized for several days. "It's a good feeling and also a lot of fun," he said, "and I know if I have a problem, they'll all be here doing it for me."

Visiting one another is another means of emotional support, especially for the elderly and chronically ill. One Amish woman told us about visiting a friend on an off-Sunday. She and her husband made the twenty-mile trip by horse and buggy on one of the coldest days of winter. When we expressed surprise at taking such a chilly journey, she said simply that their friend was recovering from cancer and needed visitors.

Expressions of care often come from beyond the local church district in the form of card showers. Contributors to Amish newspapers encourage readers to write—or in some cases, send money—to cheer ill or lonely people. "Let's have a thinking-of-you shower for Enos Yoder. He will be seventy-four March 15. He cannot do anything and has many long days," began one request. "Let's have a get well or whatever-you-wish shower for Mrs. Andy L. Hershberger," urged another. "She had hip replacement surgery. Let's fill her mailbox."[6] These showers generate scores of cards from people, many of whom the recipients will never meet because they live outside the community or state, but who reach out to fellow church members with concern and care.

What About the Wayward?

The practice of mutual aid has a flip side. The Amish, like anyone else, face the challenge of betrayal, disobedience, and offense. Coping with disobedience requires a different set of religious habits than mutual aid—rites that include confession, discipline, and shunning, all of which remind members of their spiritual responsibility to and for one another. The practice of shunning may seem harsh to outsiders, but the Amish see mutual aid and church discipline as two sides of the same coin. Both involve reciprocal relationships of accountability and respect, and both sustain community.

All human communities experience broken and tense relationships from time to time. Some twenty-first-century Americans choose anonymity, avoidance, and distance to cope when conflicts arise. Moreover, privacy fences and automatic garage doors allow people to bypass their neighbors, and career changes and divorce reflect a cultural impulse to

79

start life again. The Amish, bound in close relationships, cannot easily move away or avoid conflict. Disagreements must be addressed head-on, often publicly and in the church. And those who betray their vows to the community are not ignored.

Amish churches deal with violations of the *Ordnung* through confession and, in some cases, discipline. If the social shaming of discipline does not change an offender's attitudes and behaviors, the church may excommunicate and subsequently shun the person.[7]

Members often initiate private confession, going to a church leader to confess violations of biblical teaching (theft, fornication, lying) or of the *Ordnung* (owning a computer, filing a lawsuit, flying in an airplane). Depending on the nature of the transgression, the church official may offer loving counsel and close the matter. In other cases, he may require the individual to make a public confession, either sitting or kneeling before the entire church. The church will "subpoena" the wayward who do not come forward voluntarily, and ask them to appear before the *Gmay* to confess or at least explain their behavior, noted one Amish man.

Although bishops, ministers, and deacons oversee the process, discipline involves the entire *Gmay* during the occasional Members Meetings that follow Sunday-morning services. After the benediction, the bishop dismisses all the children and unbaptized teens, leaving sixty or so adult members. Then the work of community discipline and pardon begins.

Drawing on Matthew 18:15–20, the Amish see this task as one of the church's key responsibilities. In some ways, this authority parallels that of a Roman Catholic priest, who can pardon a repentant parishioner of sin, but the Amish believe that Matthew 18 authorizes the entire church to make decisions about membership that are binding on earth and endorsed in heaven. The sacred nature of the church's decision making is underscored in verse 20 where Jesus says, "For where two or three are gathered together in my name, there am I in the midst of them." This authority of the *gathered church*, meeting in the presence of Christ, provides divine sanction for all the decisions related to membership, the *Ordnung*, and other matters.

Decisions Endorsed in Heaven

Although Amish people view Members Meetings with solemn respect, they are also aware of their church's fallibility. They realize the church consists of people who are prone to sin, yet who sincerely seek to embody the will of God on earth. Violations of biblical teaching and the *Ordnung* are seen as sinful, but not because the *Ordnung* is an exact replication of divine will. Transgressions are sinful because, to the Amish, they signal self-centeredness and rebelliousness—in short, a disobedient heart. Aware that the Amish way is difficult for others to understand, Amos, a minister, explained, "I know it doesn't make sense to outsiders; they think, 'What's the matter with a car?' Well, nothing. It's the giving up part. That's what's important."

Giving up things not explicitly forbidden in the Bible surprises some Christians. Indeed, many outsiders would see some of what the Amish consider sins as signs of free thinking, not self-centeredness; of healthy individuality, not defiance. Such a difference points to the deep divide between Amish beliefs and mainstream values. For most Amish, it is not that important what the *Ordnung* prohibits, or even if the prohibitions were to change next year. The obedience or disobedience revealed by a person's attitude toward the church is the issue, not the details of a rule. "Remember . . . the way to heaven is paved with obedience, and the way to hell is paved with disobedience," says one minister, who had himself been subject to discipline earlier in his life.[8]

In the Members Meeting, the contrite one comes forward and confesses, "I have sinned. I earnestly beg God and the church for sincere patience with me, and from now on I will carry more concern and care with the Lord's help."[9] The bishop might then ask some questions about the offense, after which the offender may seek to explain his or her actions or may simply sob in remorse. After confessing, the person leaves the room; the bishop suggests a remedy and asks each member if he or she agrees. The vote by the members is usually unanimous.

The tearful confessions, frank discussions, and binding decisions in Members Meetings are strictly confidential, and members are forbidden from talking about them. Ministers urge church members to forgive and forget, or more precisely, to pardon and leave it in the past. In the words of an Amish historian, "A confessed sin may never be held against a person again—it is dead and buried." In fact, if a member does leak information, he or she could be disciplined for gossip.

After the vote, the offender returns to hear the verdict. He or she may be reinstated immediately or perhaps suspended from membership for six weeks, the typical punishment. If suspended, the offender meets with the ministers for admonition and attends church, but during the first sermon sits in a front row, bent over, with face in hands as a sign of remorse. After six weeks, the disciplined person is restored to membership.*

The Return of the Prodigal

The rite of restoration revolves around Jesus' parable of the prodigal son, the story of a son who shames his wealthy father by demanding his inheritance and then squandering it. After coming to his senses, he returns home, hoping merely to be taken into his father's house as a slave. Instead, he is welcomed back as a beloved child (Luke 15:11–32).

---

*The length and details of the temporary suspension vary somewhat by community.

In the same spirit, those who have been expelled, either for a short time or for a number of years, are restored to membership in the *Gmay* if they are contrite and willing to confess their errors.

Services of restoration in Amish churches occur in Members Meetings. Some include a prayer from *Christenpflicht*, "On Behalf of Those Who Have Fallen Away," which is followed by a reading of the prodigal son story. Then the bishop speaks: "If you, fallen brother or sister, stand in hope that the Heavenly Father has thus far drawn near to you and is again merciful to you, then you may in God's name kneel down." In the midst of the gathered church, surrounded by family, friends, and neighbors, the penitent one answers questions posed by the bishop:

"Do you recognize and confess that you have earned this discipline and that it has rightfully been dealt out to you?

"Do you also sincerely request patience from God and the church?

"Do you promise that you hereafter desire to live more carefully with the Lord's help, and to walk in His commandments, and help to apply them and to counsel and labor in the church in all points as you promised at the time of your baptism?"[10]

Hearing affirmative answers, the bishop announces, "In the name of the Lord and of the church, you are offered my hand, arise." The kiss of peace, the symbol that earlier had sealed the rite of baptism, is then offered to the individual.

Confession and discipline often bring healing both to individuals and to the church community. One member described a young married couple who were suspended because of their premarital sexual behavior. "They asked to be expelled, and so there was this six-week period of repentance. When they were reinstated as members it was such a sensational thing, and everybody felt that this couple really . . . was sorry for what they had done and wanted to lead a better life. Everybody felt so good about it. It was really a healthy thing for the church. It was really a good feeling."[11]

Although confession and restoration reaffirm the values of humility and submission, they are not always successful in changing behaviors, particularly those involving alcohol abuse or sexual compulsion. Repeat offenders may find themselves confessing before the *Gmay* over and over again, but unable to break addictions the church deems sinful. Some Amish churches, though not all, are open to professional mental health counseling. Such counseling in tandem with the church's rites of discipline can be a therapeutic and healing combination.

Delivering People to Satan

Occasionally a church member will directly or persistently flout the authority of the church, rejecting discipline and calls for confession. These situations, though rare, are considered quite serious, for they are a breach of baptismal vows—lifelong promises to comply with the church, made before God and a host of witnesses. Typically those who ignore the church's counsel—buying a car, for instance, and refusing to sell it—have already decided to leave. They expect to be excommunicated.

With discipline and excommunication, the church draws a sharp line between baptized members and those who have not joined the *Gmay*. Only members, because they vowed to uphold the *Ordnung* at baptism, can be excommunicated and shunned. Teenagers reared in Amish homes who haven't joined the church and eventually pursue another way of life cannot be excommunicated. They no doubt bring their parents grief, but because they never took baptismal vows, they cannot be shunned. The amount of acceptance they receive from their parents varies greatly from family to family.

Excommunication is a long-standing practice of the Catholic Church and many Protestant ones. It is similar in some ways to firing an employee who flagrantly violates company policy. Among the Amish, excommunication is affirmed by a vote of church members, but it is done only after leaders have spent weeks or months patiently urging wayward members to repent. Restoration is always the goal, but because it requires repentance, it's not always achieved.

With other avenues exhausted, a deacon and a minister deliver the church's verdict, using 1 Corinthians 5:5: "To deliver such a one unto Satan for the destruction of the flesh, that the spirit may be saved in the day of the Lord Jesus." These words sound harsh to modern ears, and certainly those expelled do not see themselves aligned with Satan. But for the Amish, holding members accountable is the flip side of the community barn raising that outsiders celebrate. Living in community requires both.

A Dose of Tough Love

Because the Amish believe that church membership is not just a private spiritual matter, expulsion from the church has social consequences. Following a practice advocated in the seventeenth-century Dordrecht Confession—a practice that Jakob Ammann invoked to spark the Amish movement in 1693—the Amish use shaming rituals after excommunication to remind everyone of the broken relationship and hopefully jolt defectors into repentance. This practice is commonly known as shunning.

Contrary to popular notions, shunning does not involve severing all social ties. Members may talk with ex-members, for example. But certain acts, such as accepting rides or money from ex-members and eating at the same table with them, are forbidden. "We still help ex-members," said one farmer, but "generally we don't invite them to social events or to weddings or to things like school meetings."

Amish church members outside the offender's *Gmay* are also expected to shun the ex-member. Members are even expected to shun an ex-member in their own household, although the spouse of an ex-member remains married to him or her, and may continue to live in the same house. A person who refuses to shun an excommunicated spouse jeopardizes his or her own standing within the church and risks the possibility of being expelled.

Although shunning is practiced by all Amish churches, its strictness varies from family to family and from one *Gmay* to another. Some *Gmay*s shun an ex-member for life or until the ex-member repents, but others stop shunning after a year if the former member joins another Anabaptist church.[12]

"Shunning is not an Amish invention or innovation," said Jesse adamantly. The Amish cite more than a half dozen New Testament scriptures in support of the practice. "If any man that is called a brother be a fornicator, or covetous, or an idolater, or a drunkard, or an extortioner," writes the apostle Paul in a text that is read at each Council Meeting, "with such a one do not eat" (1 Corinthians 5:11). In another place Paul advises Christians to "withdraw yourselves from every brother that walketh disorderly" (2 Thessalonians 3:6). Yet another New Testament passage enjoins believers to "mark them which cause divisions and offenses contrary to the doctrine which ye have learned; and avoid them" (Romans 16:17).

These texts and others lead the Amish to believe that "shunning is a practice commanded and sanctioned by God for the protection of the church."[13] In the words of Bishop Eli, "it helps to keep our church intact" by removing rebellious and disobedient voices who would stir up dissension. It also reminds offenders of their broken vows, in hopes that they will confess their errors and return to the fold.

Ex-members are always welcomed back after they confess their sin. Parents, in particular, can be persistent in begging their wayward children to return. And given their belief in the sacred nature of parenting, parents often blame themselves for a child's exit. "Oh, Irene! It gets so lonesome without you and it's hard to go on," one mother wrote to her daughter, who had left the church after baptism. "The waiting is so painful. . . . I'm very, very sorry that something like this happened."[14]

In the Amish view, shunning is tough love for the wayward. An Amish woman drew from her experience as a mother to explain its basis. "Shunning and spanking go side by side," she said. "We love our children. When we spank them, it's a discipline to help them control their minds. When spanking, we don't get angry at them, and the same is true for shunning." For the Amish, healthy churches, like good parents, mete out discipline with love. Because the Amish believe that each person's eternal soul is at stake, they contend that giving a dose of communal discipline is the most loving thing to do.

To be sure, those who are excommunicated rarely see shunning as an act of love. Wounded and frequently embittered by their experiences, they often dismiss Amish claims that the church cares for its prodigals. Books such as *True Stories of the X-Amish* and Web sites containing first-person accounts by former members sharply criticize shunning as unbiblical, vengeful acts by power-hungry elders.[15] Certainly some Amish leaders, just like leaders in other churches, do abuse their power. In other cases, even if there is no clear abuse of power, some bishops and ministers wield authority unwisely.

Yet even as the Amish acknowledge the imperfections of their disciplinary process, they are not about to abandon a tradition they believe is clearly taught in the Bible. "It should not alarm us that the world does not understand the value of scriptural discipline in the church," wrote one church leader. "What should alarm us is when we ourselves begin to question and doubt the practice of shunning unfaithful brethren."[16]

Coming Home

The concept of separating from sinners is not entirely foreign in non-Amish church life. Mainstream churches sometimes enforce separation by barring convicted sex offenders from church grounds. What outsiders find so offensive about shunning is that it applies to what the modern mind considers trivial violations of the *Ordnung*. One woman, who had married an outsider and left the Amish church, expressed exasperation as she recounted her parents' interpretation of her exit. "No matter what I might have done, I had not turned my back on [God], as my parents would frequently suggest."[17]

Occasionally ex-members do return, sometimes years later. Those who return with contrite hearts are welcomed back. They do not need to be rebaptized, but are reinstated into the church in the rite of restoration.

In 1992, one couple recounted their journey in an open letter to Amish young people. The husband had been a deacon in an Amish church in Delaware when they left. "It was very hard on my dear father and mother when we left the Amish *Gmay*," Samuel J. Beachy recalled. "They came to visit us . . . and asked us to come back."[18]

For two decades Sam and his wife, Lena, attended a different church that was active in evangelism and mission, and Sam even served as a congregational leader. But over time they were increasingly troubled by a gnawing sense of unease. Sam felt he could not teach the biblical injunction to honor one's parents because he had disrespected his own parents' wishes. On top of that, Sam and Lena became increasingly concerned that their new church was drifting closer to the world. At first, the absence of the Amish *Ordnung* had felt freeing, but the lack of guidelines soon troubled them as they saw how people in their new church accumulated possessions and raised their children.

About twenty years after leaving, they returned to the Amish church, and on bended knee were reinstated as members. "Do not think, dear friends, this was easy," Sam emphasized. "NO! NO! This was very hard on our pride, to come back . . . and give up our nice cars . . . [and] our electricity and confess we had gone the wrong direction. It cost many a tear, but it brought exceedingly great joy and peace into our hearts and lives." Sam had lost his ordination when he left the Amish, but after he returned, he was nominated for a ministry position, chosen by drawing lots, and ordained again.

Although Sam and Lena are not alone in returning to the church after years away, they are somewhat unusual. "I know it is a lot easier to go drifting with the tide of this world," Sam admitted. Still, it was precisely that worldly tide that motivated the Beachys to choose the Amish way once again. They believed they had found, in the Amish church, a community of accountability—a community that would not let them do as they please but would strengthen their affection for the things that matter most.

Part III

The Amish Way in Everyday Life

CHAPTER SEVEN

Children

Our children are the only crop we can take along to heaven.

—AMISH FATHER

W e were honored when Katie and Sammy invited us to their home for church. Many things that Sunday morning reminded us of how different Amish worship is from our own: extremely slow singing, no instrumental music, hard backless benches, two long prayers as we knelt on the floor, long sermons in a dialect we didn't understand, and more than two hundred people packed into what seemed like space for about half that number. There was no Sunday school, no nursery, no children's sermon, no praise band, no bulletin, and no announcement saying how pleased they were to have us as visitors.

Yet nothing astonished us as much as the children. For three straight hours, three- and four-year-olds sat quietly on benches and in the laps of their parents, seemingly quite content. Partway through the service, someone passed around a plate of crackers so that the children could have a small snack, and those who tired of their fathers' laps would sometimes toddle over to their mothers or grandparents. Occasionally a child left for a bathroom break. The rest of the time, however, they sat quietly, occupying themselves with simple playthings—a small doll, a handkerchief, or tiny bits of fabric or paper.

Watching the children that day reminded us that the church service is an incubator of patience, a patience rarely seen in most young children. Amish boys and girls, who can be noisy and rambunctious at play, learn this discipline at an early age. Taught and caught from infancy, patience shapes the character and spiritual disposition of Amish people, becoming the social reality they take for granted.

A Sacred Calling

To have and raise children who grow up to respect God and join the Amish church is the preeminent goal of couples. Leaders discourage artificial birth control, although some couples in change-oriented groups occasionally do use contraceptives.[1] Abortions are universally considered sin. If an unmarried woman becomes pregnant, she almost invariably weds the father if he is Amish. If he is not Amish, she may leave and marry him outside the church or remain in the community and raise the child as a single parent. But single parenthood is rare in Amish society.

Parents warmly welcome children into their homes as gifts from God. Those born with disabilities are dubbed "God's special children sent from heaven" and showered with extra loving care. Parents may adjust their work to flex with the duties of child rearing. Mothers, for example, rarely hold outside jobs when they have young children, and fathers often select jobs that enable the family to work together. "We bought a deli business in a farmers' market so the family can work together; it's a family thing," said Jesse.

One might expect that an Amish childhood would be chock-full of religious activities like vacation Bible school, religious camps, and Sunday school. Yet formal religious education is missing in an Amish child's life.[2] Fathers and mothers—not church programs, schools, or youth pastors—shoulder the duty of passing on the faith to their children.

Parents take this task seriously. Tradition holds them account-able for the spiritual outcomes of their children, even though young adults have a choice to embrace or abandon their faith. The words of Menno Simons, an early Anabaptist leader, are instructive: "Watch over their souls as long as they are under your care, lest you lose also your own salvation on their account."[3] "Every father," says the author of "Rules of a Godly Life," "must give an account for the souls of his household."[4]

Ministers frequently remind parents of their child-rearing duties with verses from a sixty-four-line poem, "Die Kinder Zucht" (The Upbringing of the Child). Those who fail in this task, the poet says, "face the danger of being a total stranger to heaven."

> When early discipline is lacking,
> Times will come which bode no good.
> Sinful nature must be tamed,
> Else conflict taints the neighborhood.
>
> What you teach them early on,
> They'll later bring to mind.
> Habit has tremendous strength;
> Both the good and the evil kind.[5]

Raising children who join the church increases one's status in the Amish community. This respect diminishes if children forsake the

Amish way, and parents may feel as though they have failed. Some parents fear for the salvation of such children, especially if a wayward son or daughter rejects Christianity entirely. In situations where adult children choose to join a different denomination, parental reactions vary. Some may mix regret with a sense of comfort that their children and grandchildren are at least attending a church.

In any case, parenting is considered a divine calling. One mother summarized its spiritual significance in a poem she penned after hearing a minister preach on the qualifications for ordained ministers. He reminded his listeners that motherhood was a sacred calling no less significant than church leadership itself.

> Then the words of the visiting preacher
> Struck my heart like a two-edged sword,
> For he asked, "What's the highest calling
> Ever given to man by the Lord?"
> He went on and said, "You mothers
> At home with your children so small,
> Yours is a very great calling,
> Yours is a most sacred call.
>
> I lowered my head in submission,
> For the lot had fallen on me
> To carry this most precious calling,
> For I am a mother, you see.[6]

Living in a patriarchal society, this woman—and the minister she quotes—underscore the esteemed value of mothers in the spiritual realm.

Although mothers and fathers take the lead, they receive lots of help from other adults. Children's spiritual beliefs, practices, and affections are molded as they watch adults around them and join in rituals of faith—sitting quietly through three-hour church services, singing, kneeling, and hearing spiritual wisdom from adults. Children learn by observing and mimicking the behavior of dozens of Amish people— older siblings, aunts, uncles, cousins, and neighbors—in the course of everyday living. Parents would heartily agree that it takes all the people in the proverbial village to help them raise their children well.

Singing Their Way Through Childhood

Songs, prayers, and nursery rhymes nurture children in the Amish way at an early age. "I myself was taught to sing early in my childhood," says Sarah, who considers it her motherly duty to train her children to sing. "We as parents are responsible to openly teach our children about God, the Supreme Being, and drill into their minds fitting music for the soul." [7]

Bedtime prayers and songs help form the spiritual character of children. The Lord's Prayer is one of the first things many children memorize, usually in German and English, by the time they're four or five years old. "The Lord's Prayer was the first thing I learned at the age of five," said Mary, a mother of seven. "My husband quotes it when he puts the children to bed, and they could quote it before they went to school." Jesse told us that "Miede bin ich, geh sur ruh" is "a good bed-time rhyme that everybody knows."

> I'm tired and I'm going to bed. Close my eyes up tight.
> Father, may those angels of yours watch over me tonight.
> If I have done some wrong today, please, God, look upon
> my sorrow;
> Your grace in Christ's blood, can prepare me for tomorrow. [8]

Sam Stoltzfus writes that, in his childhood, "There was always prayer, from infant age on. Our parents taught us to put our hands under the table and pray a silent table prayer six times a day, before and after each meal. Then there was the evening prayer that Dad would read for the whole family just before bedtime. . . . There was a secure feeling in our hearts when we would go up the stairs to our beds." In a world of many perils, "we felt protected all night long."[9]

These practices of song and prayer attune children to God and also bond family members across generations. Sarah describes her joy in hearing her young children sing: "How the words touched my heart as they flowed from the lips of our three-year-old, 'Wo ist Jesus, mein Verlangen, mein geliebter Herr und Freund?' Where is Jesus whom I long for, my beloved Lord and friend?" She then adds that "Grandma taught this hymn to our oldest son in his early years, and it keeps on being passed down to our babies, one by one as soon as they're old enough to lisp the words." Her family also sings the *Loblied*, the second hymn in every church service. "Although our oldest children couldn't always carry a tune," Sarah explains, "it didn't seem to bother them at all. They just said the words, supplying their own tune."[10]

Significantly, many of the songs that children first learn to sing focus on God's love and care. Two of the most widely sung are "Gott ist die Liebe" ("God Is Love") and "Jesus Liebt die Kleine Kinder" ("Jesus Loves the Little Children"). Another favorite in some families is "Ich hab ein Freund" (I have a friend who loves me . . . and that friend is Jesus).

When young children begin school they learn songs that, beyond educating them about God's love, help train them in the Amish way.

If kind to all your classmates, obedient to the rule,
If studious and thoughtful, you're spelling love at school.[11]

It's the Spanking

When one Amish grandmother was asked, "What are the most important things to teach children?" she answered succinctly: "To work and to obey."[12] Although these words might show up on a list of child-rearing goals in other North American households, they'd hardly be at the top. In any case, the matter-of-factness with which this grandmother answered the question reveals how highly these traits are valued in Amish life.

For many Americans, the phrase *obedience training* applies mostly to dogs. In Amish society, it pertains to people, beginning with children. Amish child-rearing literature abounds with references to obedience, not as a control button for authoritarian parents, but because obedience is a core value of their faith. Disobedience is a sin, a signpost on the road to eternal damnation. Jesus obeyed God, and his followers are expected to obey God as well.

Most Christians would agree, and they may even add that children are expected to obey their parents. But Amish understandings of obedience go a big step further: church members are expected to abide by the regulations of the church, thereby guarding their salvation. By teaching their children the habits of obedience, parents place them on the road to heaven and safeguard them from hell.

One spring morning we visited with Hannah, a mother of seven. Having just cleaned up from weeding the garden, she invited us into her living room, where we talked about child rearing. We told her that some of our friends who are dentists, nurses, and doctors say that, compared to many non-Amish children they encounter, Amish offspring are quiet, well mannered, and well behaved. "Why might that be?" we asked. Without hesitation or a trace of humor, Hannah responded, "Oh, it's the spanking that makes them so nice."

99

Hannah explained that, when children are about two years old, their wills need to be broken. If it's not done at that stage, she said, they will likely become disobedient and rebellious adults. The spanking helps correct them and "make them nice." Another mother explained that when children are old enough to fold their hands at prayer time, they are also old enough to be reprimanded with light spanks when disobedient.

Amish parents turn to the words of King Solomon to support corporal discipline: "He that spareth his rod hateth his son; but he that loveth him chasteneth him betimes" (Proverbs 13:24). Looking to the New Testament, they cite the observation in the book of Hebrews that God disciplines Christians the way a father disciplines a son. "No chastening for the present seemeth to be joyous, [but] . . . afterward it yieldeth the peaceable fruit of righteousness" (Hebrews 12:11).

Parents are quick to say, however, that spanking and other forms of physical discipline must never be done in anger or frustration. "Is there a wrong time to punish a child?" asks one Amish handbook on the Christian life. "Yes, when you are angry, [so] unless it hurts you more than the child, stop at once until you can discipline in a spirit of love."[13] The child should understand the reason for discipline, too, so that "punishment ends on a happy note, sweet and forgiving," says Naomi, a mother writing about discipline. Because correction ultimately "leads to happiness . . . [discipline] must be the result of our love for the child's happiness, both now and in the hereafter."[14]

These links—between spanking, happiness, and heaven—provide the framework for Amish child discipline, an approach that nurtures obedience instead of individuality, and conformity instead of creativity. It's a framework that many Americans find disturbing and perhaps even abusive. Naomi disagrees. In fact, she believes that letting children go without discipline is "the cruelest kind of child abuse." She poses the question rhetorically: "Now wouldn't it be abusive above all abuses to withhold from our children the training they need for a life of discipline and self-control, of service to God?"

Fleeing the Devil's Workshop

In an essay titled "Tips on Training a Two-Year-Old," Lavina, an Amish mother, offers advice on teaching toddlers to work. "If you are packing daddy's lunch, set your child on the countertop and let her help. . . . Explain that the cookie is for daddy's snack this afternoon. . . . Two-year-olds can be taught to set the table. . . . Our oldest was able to set ours in the morning before dad came in from chores."[15]

Although work nears the top of the Amish child-rearing agenda, its tie to eternal life is more tenuous than that of obedience. Amish people frequently cite an Old Testament verse about working by the sweat of one's brow to produce food (Genesis 3:19). A prominent proverb, "Idleness is the devil's workshop," often enters Amish conversation, and the widely read "Rules of a Godly Life" claims that "idleness is a resting-pillow of the devil and a cause of all sorts of wickedness." Never let the devil "find you idle," for he has great power "over the slothful, to plunge them into all kinds of sins, for idleness gives rise to every vice."[16]

Amish people believe that work is a spiritual discipline that shields them from sin and vice. Whether their work ethic is a by-product of their rural lifestyle or is grounded in the belief that God holds them accountable for how they use their time, they universally agree that hard work is virtuous and sloth is not. "We mistrust a soft and leisurely life," write sheep farmers Chris and Rachel Stoll. "We want to keep our children from becoming soft and lazy."[17]

Children learn this discipline at an early age. One store owner who grew up on a farm said, "We boys used to think that our dad actually planted some weeds for us to pull, just to keep us out of mischief!"

In her article about training two-year-olds, Lavina offers other ways to get young children involved in household tasks: cleaning, dusting, sweeping, and even sewing with a large needle and thread. "Two-year-olds love to help with the dishes! I know this takes a lot of 'dying to self,' but then what job doesn't? . . . It's surprising how they remember the details at age eight if they are taught properly when they are two." She also explains how she receives help from a two-year-old to care for a newborn. "Two-year-olds enjoy helping with baby, too. Have them bring a clean diaper, hand you the powder box, and then put the wet diaper into the bucket."[18]

Teaching children to work has been, in some ways, an economic necessity in Amish life. Farming is labor-intensive, especially for families who must forgo tractors and automated machinery. Yet even those who work off the farm praise the discipline of hard work. More than a means for earning money and getting things done, work is considered virtue training, bending children's affections in a godly direction. "It's too late to teach children to work after they're through school" is a common adage, and such teaching cannot begin too early. "Children are involved from little on up," one woodshop owner explained. "From the time they could stand on a five-gallon bucket, they're up looking and watching what you're doing."[19]

Reading, 'Riting, 'Rithmetic, and Religion

Although children in a few Amish communities attend public schools, the vast majority of them attend Amish schools. These private schools, operated by parents, do not have formal classes on religion, but they promote religious values at many turns: singing a hymn to open each school day, reciting the Lord's Prayer, teaching obedience and cooperation, and reading stories with flashbacks to Anabaptist history. A handbook for

Amish schools explains, "It is our aim to teach religion all day long in our curriculum and on the playground: in arithmetic by accuracy (no cheating), in English by learning to say what we mean, in history by humanity (kindness and mercy), in health by teaching cleanliness and thriftiness, in geography by learning to make an honest living on the soil, in music by singing praises to God, on the school ground by teaching honesty, respect, sincerity, humbleness, and yes, the Golden Rule."[20]

Children also learn about the Amish way through songs, poetry, and proverbs, which are all parts of the "hidden curriculum" that passes Amish faith across the generations. One favorite schoolroom verse captures core aspects of Amish spirituality:

I must be a Christian child,
Gentle, patient, meek, and mild,
Must be honest, simple, true.
I must cheerfully obey,
Giving up my will and way. . . .

"Giving up my will and way" are code words for *uffgevva*, and teachers often note that the middle letter in *pride* is *I*. In the classroom and at play, children learn to esteem others above themselves and take in the religious values of their community.

Of course, Amish education lacks certain things that many people value: university-trained teachers, an expansive curriculum, computers with high-speed Internet access, and up-to-date science labs. Moreover, in a one-room school with about two dozen children from eight or ten families in the immediate neighborhood, there is little diversity of thought, no ethnic or racial diversity, and no exposure to other faiths. But the Amish prefer it this way. For them, it's better to have a teacher steeped in Amish values than one trained in the latest educational techniques, and it's better to instill certain spiritual values in children than let them explore the world and all its options. Not everyone would want their children to be so sheltered, but the Amish find it far superior to the alternative. Amish schools thus complement the efforts of parents to pass along the Amish way.

Habit-Forming Practices

In an essay titled "Our Plain Folks and Their Spirituality," published in a monthly magazine for Amish readers, retired farmer and grandfather Sam Stoltzfus explains how children learn the Amish way: "Our spiritual life begins [in] childhood . . . the babies go along to church when they are six weeks old."[21]

Sam thinks faith is communicated by actions more than words. "We saw by example how our parents planned their lives and how much time they devoted to helping others. . . . I can well recall mother making a hearty meal for hobos who came to our house. Many times we saw dad rush off to barn raisings or take his team [of horses] to plow for a sick neighbor." Sam also watched his dad give generously to needy people in the church and prepare alms money for communion. Even the children were expected to give to the church.

Sarah, a generation younger than Sam, underscores the importance of repetition in shaping children's beliefs and affections. Drawing on her experience of teaching her children to sing, she agrees with Sam that early training can make all the difference. "Repetition of the words, the tunes, the feelings will plant something into our hearts that will remain there for life," she writes. "What we learned in our tender years will still be there, reminding us of what is right."[22]

Sam remembers his deep desire as a nine-year-old to "go in with the boys" as church members entered a house or barn for *Gmay*, rather than walking in with his parents as young children did. "It was a big ritual in our Amish world," he says, "the first rite of passage from boy-hood to being big." He had already memorized the Lord's Prayer as a six-year-old, but his mother insisted that he memorize the *Loblied* with its "four verses with seven lines each—over 140 words and all in High German" before he could walk into church with the big boys and sit with them. "Finally," he recalls, "I could say the whole twenty-eight lines without missing a syllable. Mother smiled and said, 'Now you may go in with the boys.' How important I felt walking in with the boys that first time. . . . There we'd sit, me and Manny Beiler, holding the *Ausbund* hymnbook together. Then when the *Loblied* was sung I could read the lines and help sing."[23]

The habits, practices, and rituals of Amish life shape the spiritual character of children in profound ways. They are not permitted to decide for themselves whether or not to go to church or whether or not to kneel for family prayers. Parents prescribe the Amish way by example and ritual, and children are expected to walk in this way until they come of age in their late teens. They learn the habits of silence and patience at *Gmay* by observing scores of people practice them for three hours every other Sunday. They learn obedience because it is reinforced by teachers, parents, and preachers, who all send the same message: disobedience is sin. All of their friends, associates, and kin follow simi-lar practices and rituals, etching into their minds the beliefs and affec-tions of their spiritual world.

These practices, learned in the early years, lay the foundation for a patient faith in a perilous world. And when children grow up, they pass these same practices on to their own children, by example and word, as they gather around their kitchen tables day after day.

CHAPTER EIGHT

Family

The kitchen table is the most important piece
of furniture in an Amish house.

—AMISH PARENT

W e visit many Amish families in the course of our research, and some of them invite us to lodge in their homes. Without exception they ask us to join them in their morning and evening prayers.

On one occasion we stayed with Amos and Anna, parents of eight and owners of a manufacturing firm that distributes horse-drawn farm equipment worldwide. That evening, we gathered around the oak table in the center of their spacious kitchen to eat popcorn and ice cream. Their children peppered us with questions about our research and travels. At about 9:00 P.M. one of the older boys signaled to his father, and a few minutes later, Amos cleared his throat: "Two of our boys need to leave by 5:00 A.M. tomorrow to help a neighbor set up for an auction, so let's have our evening prayer now so they can go to bed."

Silence fell quickly as we knelt on the floor, resting our hands on chairs we had pushed back from the table. Anna handed Amos *Christenpflicht*. He turned some pages and then raised his voice as he read an evening prayer in German:

> O Lord God, kind and merciful Father, this day Thou . . . gaveth us another opportunity to serve Thee and to grow in godliness. . . . Forgive us, Lord, where we have sinned against Thee. . . . O holy and merciful Father, let the light of Thy loving kindness illuminate our pathway. . . . Protect us with Thy great power and watch over us, for we are Thy creation, the work of Thy hands. Prepare us for Thy eternal salvation. . . . Amen."[1]

Amos closed with the Lord's Prayer, "Our Father which art in heaven . . . ," and we all joined in German. The tick-tock of a clock in the next room filled the silence as the prayer ended. The two boys headed upstairs, and we returned to our seats and resumed chatting for another hour.

Visiting in the home of Eli and Fannie in Ohio, we awoke one morning at 5:30 A.M. to the sound of dishes being set on the table. Eli, a minister, operates a business that cleans and repackages canned foods for resale in "bent-and-dent" stores. As dawn was breaking, we gathered around the kitchen table for breakfast and morning prayers. A gaslight hanging over the kitchen table sputtered softly as Eli read a chapter of scripture. Then, pushing back our chairs, we knelt as he read a morning prayer from *Christenpflicht*:

> O God and Father of all light and comfort, Thy mercies are new every morning and great is Thy faithfulness. We praise and honor Thee for this new day. . . . Keep us free of all superstition, idolatry, pride and disobedience. . . . Teach us to act according to Thy will, for we are Thy children. . . . Guide us upon paths of righteousness. . . . Encompass us with Thy grace and keep Thy hand over us at all times. . . . Amen.

Amish family life is bracketed by prayers such as these, which are said around the kitchen table at the opening and closing of the day. There are, of course, many other occasions outside regular church services for prayers, songs, and devotional experiences. Many of these moments occur in the home, making it an important crucible for spiritual development.

Prayerful Rhythms

Amish life beats to the rhythm of many three-hundred-year-old prayers. The words anchor people in their heritage, link them to their ancestors, and remind them of God's eternal presence. The prayers open a window into Amish faith: the kneeling posture of humility, the surrender of *uffgevva*, the togetherness of family, the spiritual leadership of the father, the home as a spiritual hearth, and the abiding respect for voices from the past. The repetition of the prayers etches reverence into the children's hearts and sustains the adults' spiritual commitments.

In addition to their morning prayer, older couples with more relaxed schedules may include scripture or devotional readings in their routines. Evening prayer patterns also vary somewhat by family. "Ruthie usually reads Bible stories to the smaller children before they go to bed," explained Jesse. "The mother definitely carries the most responsibility to nurture and teach young children. . . . She just has that special connection with them." Some parents pray together after the children are in bed, but other families include their children in evening prayers. In some families the father always reads a prayer; in others, family members take turns reading a prayer or offering one of their own.

Beyond the kneeling prayers, silent prayers open and close each meal as the family sits around the table. Some people pray the Lord's

Prayer silently as their mealtime prayer, reflected one man, "because it says, 'Give us this day our daily bread.'" For others, the silent mealtime prayers provide opportunities to express gratitude for God's faithfulness. Stretching over several minutes, silent prayers insert the habit of patience into each day.

The increase in nonfarm employment has disrupted morning prayers for some families. "In shop families," explained one father, "too often everyone grabs a quick breakfast, a lunch pail, and then heads out the door." Family members who operate stands at farmers' markets—selling such items as produce, baked goods, flowers, and candy—may leave home by 4:00 A.M. to arrive at their stands by 7:00. Likewise, carpenters on construction crews often leave home at 5:00 A.M. Even as occupational changes have disturbed some morning prayer routines, the evening ones remain largely intact. Families may adjust these evening prayer times somewhat, but they hold tightly to the practice in some form.

Seeking Still Waters

The Amish place a lower priority on individual devotional practices than some religious traditions do, and they are more inclined to value communal and family spiritual practices. Still, they do encourage private devotional practices, including prayer, fasting, and reading the Bible as well as other resources.

The Lord's Prayer is the cornerstone of prayer life because personal prayers are rarely composed or said aloud. "We don't think we can improve on Jesus' prayer," one young carpenter told us, adding that the Lord's Prayer is "a well-rounded prayer with all the key points in it." Trying to improve on the words of Jesus, in Amish minds, would be prideful and arrogant. A key phrase in this oft-repeated prayer becomes a daily reminder of the need to yield to God's divine providence: "Thy kingdom come, *Thy will be done*, in earth as it is in heaven" (Matthew 6:10, emphasis added).

Fasting, going without food for at least part of a day, is another spiritual practice for church members. Although the specific days vary by community, a fast may occur on the off-Sunday between Council Meeting and Communion Sunday. Other fast days may include Good Friday, January 6 (Old Christmas, or Epiphany), and October 11 (the traditional German holiday Michaelmas) in some communities. Fasts typically involve skipping breakfast, meditating quietly, and refraining from work. Regular activities resume with the noon meal.

Along with prayer and fasting, Amish people read devotional texts of various sorts. In addition to "Rules of a Godly Life," some people read a short, daily devotional message from such publications as *Beside Still Waters* or *Our Daily Bread*. Another non-Amish favorite is Oswald Chambers's *My Utmost for His Highest*, first published in 1927. Their use of these devotional guides, even "Rules of a Godly Life," shows that the Amish are willing to borrow spiritual resources from other religious traditions.

Of course, the most important devotional text for the Amish— the Bible—is not exclusively their own either, although the type of Bible many families read is peculiar in twentieth-first-century America: a German-English version with parallel columns of King James English and Martin Luther's German. Sometimes, while preaching, ministers will encourage members to "read a verse when you get home. You will probably understand it more that way." One minister, however, cautions that "Bible reading and study is not good when you do it to find fault and criticize churches and people around you. There is a big difference between reading for your daily bread and inspiration, and studying the Bible just to be critical of others or to justify your own contentious and rebellious thoughts."

Sunday Routines

Sunday marks the religious high point of an Amish family's week. It is a day of worship, rest, and reverence. Apart from preparing meals and caring for animals, work ceases. Businesses prominently post signs saying "No Sunday Sales." Anything that can just as easily be done on Saturday or Monday is strongly discouraged on Sunday. Buying or selling products is taboo. Going to a restaurant on Saturday is fine; on Sunday it is unthinkable. Traveling on Sunday by hired van is discouraged unless it's necessary for hospital visits or long-distance trips for funerals or weddings. Even then the hired driver might not be paid until Monday to prevent the exchange of money on Sunday.

Each district holds church services every other week. On the off-Sundays, families may attend the worship service in another district or have a quiet, slow morning at home. "We have the Amish version of Sunday school *rum die Tisch*, 'around the table,'" said Jesse. "The kitchen table is the most important piece of furniture in an Amish house. That's where we gather for meals, to read in the evenings, for Sunday devotions, and just to talk." In many non-Amish homes, the entertainment center claims that distinction.

Before breakfast on off-Sundays, families kneel for prayer around the table. "Everybody kneels down, and I read a morning prayer from *Christenpflicht* or *Lust Gärtlein*," explained Jesse. "After I read it, we give everybody a chance to say a little prayer, to say whatever's on their mind. They don't have to say anything except an 'Amen' at the end. Then we have breakfast about nine o'clock."

"After that," he continued, "we read the scriptures assigned for church the next Sunday. We go around the table and take turns with each one reading five verses. We read the chapter first in German and then go around again and read it in English. Then we talk about it and answer any questions the children have. And then sing some songs." Families sing from the *Ausbund* or other religious hymnbooks. How many songs they sing often depends on that particular family's musical ability. Poking fun at his own family's modest abilities, Jesse laughed, "We sing our best in the shower!"

In most Amish homes, a sense of quiet devotion fills morning routines on off-Sundays. It's a time for individual Bible study, reading of devotional books, and more general reading. "For me it's a time of recovery," said Jesse. After the noon meal, young children often play in the yard while older ones play softball, toss a football, or go sledding or hiking in season. During inclement weather, table games and reading are popular activities. On Sunday afternoons and evenings, families often visit shut-ins, friends who have lost loved ones, or parents with new babies. In these ways, Sundays serve to strengthen the bonds of community.

Singing: An Antidote for Depression

Most of the songs in Amish life have religious themes, but not all of them are slow-paced *Ausbund* hymns. People sing in German and English while doing household chores and visiting in one another's homes, and teenagers sing when they gather to socialize on Sunday evenings. "We sing everywhere," Jesse noted enthusiastically, "doing chores, playing, in the bathtub, at school, at reunions, for shut-ins, and sometimes with our *Rumspringa* buddies. . . . When church meets around Christmas, people often come back in the evening to the place that had church that day just to sing together."

Singing begins with childhood lullabies and extends to the final graveside hymn. Children attending Amish schools sing during opening

113

exercises each day, for Christmas programs, for family days, and for special visitors. Young people sing with gusto in German and English at Sunday-evening singings and many other gatherings. Wedding festivities feature abundant and vibrant singing. Amish people also sing at family gatherings and frolics, and during ordinary work.*

Some Amish communities have become fond of *Heartland Hymns*, a collection of five hundred songs published by an Amish woman in 2005.[2] It is popular with families and used in almost any gatherings other than church services, where the *Ausbund* is used exclusively. Having a copy of *Heartland Hymns* is "one of the litmus tests for being Amish around here," joked Jesse, as he showed us the book's contents. The vast majority of the songs are in English, although some are in German. The repertoire includes gospel songs such as "In the Rifted Rock I'm Resting," as well as more traditional hymns, such as Charles Wesley's "Love Divine, All Loves Excelling." Others might be considered lighter, country gospel: "Keep on the Sunny Side of Life," "How Far Is Heaven," and "Daddy's Hands." Apart from a few *Ausbund* hymns, *Heartland*'s selections have musical scores with shaped notes for singing four-part harmony.

The popularity of this book and similar ones used in other communities signals the growing use of English and four-part harmony in Amish singing, although unison singing remains the standard in church services. Unison singing welcomes everyone's voice, reinforces equality, and unites the entire community.

Some Amish people can read music, but most sing without any musical training. "Singing for the Amish has never been a question of singing the pitches accurately or 'in tune,'" musicologist Hilde Binford

---

*Musical instruments are not used because the Amish fear that they would call attention to the performance skills of individuals and diminish the quality of communal participation in worship. An Amish handbook notes that Jesus and the apostles didn't use musical instruments and that instruments tend to distract from the spirit of simplicity.

observes. "What has been important is that *everyone* sing, from the special children, including the severely disabled and deaf, to the elderly and infirm. They look to the martyrs, who sang on their way to death and believe that all should sing what is in their hearts."[3] For Jesse, "Singing is a really important spiritual expression. I've heard it said already, 'It's the best antidote to depression.' You can just feel the power of community when you're singing, everybody together, everyone participating. Each voice is just as important as others, even if you can't sing."

A Five-Minute Wedding

Sunday-evening singings are gatherings where young men and women meet and often begin courting. The Amish church does not arrange marriages, but both the bride and groom must be church members before a bishop will consent to marry them. This restriction is rooted in the apostle Paul's warning, "Be ye not unequally yoked together with unbelievers" (2 Corinthians 6:14). Only couples planning to leave the church would ever consider a nonchurch wedding.

Next to baptism and communion, weddings are the most important church ritual because they underscore the spiritual status of marriage and its promise of procreation. The bubbling excitement and festive atmosphere surrounding a wedding highlight its significance.[4] Yet at nearly every turn, Amish weddings resist the practices of the larger culture. Unlike customized ceremonies crafted by modern couples—with the help of wedding planners, caterers, photographers, and a teeming wedding industry—Amish weddings are the spiritual property of the church, not the couple.

Weddings are typically held on weekdays in a house or shop at the home of the bride or a nearby relative. In some instances, communities hold Saturday weddings to accommodate Amish guests who work for non-Amish employers and have a hard time taking off a day in the middle of the week. Friends and family from out of state may travel by train, van, or bus to attend. There is never a rehearsal, because the ceremonial steps are well known and require no practice.

The actual wedding ceremony comes near the end of a three-hour worship service, and it lasts only five minutes. Two couples who accompany the bride and groom constitute the entire wedding party. Although the participants wear new clothing, it is the same style they wear to church. The music consists of *Ausbund* hymns sung by the congregation. During the first song, the couple meets privately with the ministers for twenty minutes before returning to the service to wait for the five minutes that will launch their married lives.[5]

At the core of these five minutes lie the wedding vows. These promises seal an eternal bond because divorce, considered a sin, is forbidden. And, in keeping with the dictates of 1 Corinthians 7:11, the Amish believe that if a person ever leaves his or her spouse, the remaining one may not remarry until the death of the wayward one. The vows are based on these two questions:

"Do you promise that if he/she should be afflicted with bodily weakness, sickness, or some similar circumstance, that you will care for him/her as is fitting for a Christian husband/wife?

"Do you solemnly promise with one another that you will love and bear and be patient with each other, and not separate from each other until the dear God shall part you from each other through death?"[6]

After making their vows, the couple returns to their seats without a kiss or any other display of affection. The long service concludes with a lengthy kneeling prayer, and then the post-wedding festivities begin.

Despite the sober tone of the ceremony, the day is a joyous time of food and fellowship for the couple and their several hundred guests. A bounteous noon meal, eaten in several shifts, is followed by visiting, games, and singing throughout the afternoon. After supper, the festivities, which in some locales include square dancing for unmarried youth, may continue until midnight. To orchestrate this large gathering and prepare two meals without a catering service requires an enormous outpouring of free labor. Family, friends, and members of the local *Gmay* prepare the property, provide food, and take on various roles—cooks, ushers, waiters, dishwashers, table setters, and hostlers—throughout the day.

Without rehearsal dinners, photographers, candles, flowers, gowns, veils, tuxedos, rings, and expensive clothing, Amish weddings underscore the most important things in Amish life: community, simplicity, and faith. The absence of special clothing and fancy decorations on such a significant day may strike some as strange, but the Amish are convinced that these absences direct their affections toward life's most important things. To them, simple weddings are sufficiently special.

"Men and Women Aren't the Same"

Gender roles are well defined in Amish life and are based on their reading of the New Testament. The Amish take literally Paul's admonition to the Ephesians that "the husband is the head of the wife, even as Christ is the head of the church" (Ephesians 5:23). According to one Amish handbook, this means that husbands are responsible "to provide for the material and spiritual nurture of their wife and children" and "to be an example of Christian conduct." The same handbook adds that the husband is to be "the primary decision maker" in the home.[7] "My husband would not do anything without my okay," says one woman, "but I still think he's got the final say."[8]

Except in cases where the husband has died or become severely disabled, the head of an Amish family is always a man. Amish men demonstrate their family leadership in a number of areas. As we have seen, family devotional practices such as prayers and scripture readings are typically led by the father, except when young children are the focus. The husband usually takes the lead in dealing with outsiders. Although most schoolteachers are women, the trustees who oversee the schools are invariably men. Most other committees in Amish communities are composed entirely of men.

An Amish wife is to be "subject to her husband" and "help and support her husband in every way." Much of her help comes in the domestic sphere. Women perform an array of household activities: growing and preserving fruits and vegetables, making meals, sewing clothing, and tending the house, lawn, and garden. Most wives give birth to numerous children and care for their spiritual and physical well-being. Some own and operate businesses, though usually not until their children have completed school. Until that time women are "keepers at home," devoted to the welfare of their families and responsible for the day-to-day management of their households. One Amish handbook on the Christian life notes that "it is one of Satan's lies to make us think that a career outside the home would be more fulfilling" than a life devoted to homemaking.[9]

Many non-Amish people find such a comment offensive and wonder whether Amish women feel restricted in a culture of such close-cinched gender roles. Some may, but for most, their lifelong schooling in this aspect of the Amish way means that girls—and boys—are socialized into what to expect for their lives as adults. After conducting interviews with thirty Amish women in eastern Ohio, one research team concluded that all the women believed that men and women were intended to fill different roles. "Face it, men and women aren't the same," said one woman whose views were widely shared. "There are things that men are better at and things that women are better at. So I don't really understand what supposedly is the advantage of getting the roles mixed up."[10]

Although each woman in this study approved of distinct gender roles for men and women, some admitted that male headship took oppressive forms in certain households. "It definitely depends on the husband," said one woman. "Some men just have the idea . . . you know, they interpret the Bible wrong. . . . It says the husband should be the head of the household, and they think he should be the lord of the household." These particular Amish men, she concluded, "have no respect for their women. . . . And that gets passed down from generation to generation."

In addition to shaping household realities, the authority invested in men by scripture and tradition has, in some instances, slowed church leaders' willingness to address instances of domestic violence. In fact, a few years ago, a group of Amish women in one community, calling itself the Sewing Circle, compiled a booklet offering help to women in such situations.[11] The existence of this publication is a poignant note that this community, known for its gentle ways, is not completely free of violence.

Still, most Amish women with whom we spoke attest to feeling validated by their husbands and their communities. This validation derives both from their contribution to their families' economic well-being and from their recognized status before God. One study confirmed this validation of personal worth. It found that 97 percent of both Amish and non-Amish women surveyed in the same region agreed with this statement: "I am a person of worth, at least on an equal basis with others."[12]

Although a wife is to be subject to her husband, her first commitment is to God. At Council Meeting, she decides as an individual if her heart is ready for communion. She has an equal vote in church business meetings and nominates candidates for church leadership roles. With these things in mind, two scholars assert that Amish religion both supports patriarchy and blunts its most damaging aspects. For although Amish women are limited in terms of opportunities, they are "generally protected from the abuses often suffered by their non-Amish sisters, and their voices are heard and respected."[13]

Moreover, Amish couples demonstrate many signs of love and affection. One couple cites these humorous lines in praise of hugging:

> Hugging is healthy. It helps the body's immune system. It cures depression. It reduces stress. It's invigorating. It's rejuvenating. It has no unpleasant side effects.
>
> Hugging is all natural, organic, naturally sweet, and is 100% wholesome. It contains no pesticides, no preservatives, and no artificial ingredients.
>
> There are no movable parts, no batteries to wear out, no periodic checkups, no insurance requirements, and no monthly payments. It is inflation-proof, non-fattening, theft-proof, non-taxable, non-polluting, and is, of course, fully returnable.[14]

Although some Amish marriages are devoid of warmth, bound together only by the church's no-divorce policy, most people find their marriages satisfying—clear, if somewhat imperfect, reflections of Christ's love for the church (Ephesians 5:25).

Mingling Across the Generations

One day we were guests of an Amish grandmother, who lives in a *Dawdyhaus* apartment attached to the home of her married daughter. During our visit, her granddaughters knocked on the common door several times. "Grandma, may we borrow some of your cinnamon?" the six-year-old inquired at one point. "They come over a lot," Sally told us, "but it's probably a little more today because they're always curious to see my visitors."

It's impossible to exaggerate the sweep of the extended family's influence on the spiritual life of Amish society. A typical thirty-five-year-old married woman is rooted in an extended family network of about 250 adults—parents, siblings, in-laws, first cousins, aunts, and uncles. Children grow up in this thick family web, which plays a crucial role in fortifying Amish faith.

Not all Amish grandchildren have the easy access to their grandparents that Sally's grandchildren do. But those who live within walking distance spend time together tilling the garden, weeding flower beds, working in the shop, or helping with a hobby. Because Amish grandparents do not live in retirement communities, most of them see some of their grandchildren or great-grandchildren on a daily basis.

"Since Daddy is on the minister's bench at church," says one mother, "the boys sit with Grandpa [on Sunday mornings]. At his side they learned to follow the lines from the *Ausbund*. How thankful I am for our children's grandparents!"[15] Sixty-year-old Sam's grandparents lived in the *Dawdyhaus* at his home when he was young, and he remembers, "Grandmother often told us about God and Jesus. I can hear her like yesterday, singing hymns in German and English."[16]

Extended families gather to celebrate birthdays and Christmas; adult siblings help one another harvest vegetables, clean in preparation for hosting church, cut rags for weaving rugs, or construct an addition to a house or barn. Much visiting also occurs spontaneously when relatives drop in at one another's homes or meet at reunions, auctions, quilting parties, picnics, or holiday gatherings.

"We need this mingling of the generations," one grandfather muses. "It's tremendously gratifying for the elderly to walk and talk on an everyday basis with those they hold dear. . . . We have few greater joys than to see our children work side-by-side with one of their grandparents." He then derides the modern impulse "to pigeonhole

everything" into a "streamlined system that can be as cold as it is effi-
cient, [with] the old and infirmed placed in homes for the elderly,"
while everyone else goes his or her own way.[17]

This web of intergenerational relationships—children growing
up next to grandparents, with aunts and uncles all around—is one
aspect of Amish life that many outsiders envy, and perhaps idealize.
Amish people would be the first to admit that living close to so many
family members presents its share of challenges. Along with those challenges, however, come spiritual blessings, because mingling across the
generations reinforces the distinctive beliefs, practices, and affections
of Amish life.

By living with, talking to, and observing their parents and grandparents, Amish children learn about devotional practices, Sunday
routines, gender roles, and many other aspects of the Amish way. As
we will see in the next chapter, they even learn about the realm of
possessions—what to buy, what to wear, and what to forgo entirely.

CHAPTER NINE

Possessions

We say "no thanks" to the dishwasher.

—AMISH LEADER[1]

B rimming with many children, most Amish homes produce eight or more sets of dirty dishes three times a day. That means at least twenty-four glasses, dozens of plates, and countless pieces of silverware, not to mention pots, pans, mixing bowls, platters, and serving utensils. Just the perfect place for an automatic dishwasher, right?

But you will not find a dishwasher in any Amish home. "We don't believe in dirty dishes," writes Elmo Stoll, explaining why these labor-saving devices are missing from Amish kitchens. "We just work a little harder to get the task done."

The Amish ban dishwashers and other standard appliances for four reasons, according to Stoll in *Strangers and Pilgrims: Why We Live Simply*. First, he says, Amish people see themselves as travelers on a journey, headed toward eternity. "If we meant to stay here, it would make sense to accumulate and enjoy all the earthly comforts. [But] this is vanity.

We came into this world with nothing, and we are going to leave it the same way."

Love for neighbor provides a second reason for living a simple life. "How can I eat cake, when my neighbor does not have bread?" Stoll continues. "How can I discard serviceable clothing because it is not in style, when my neighbor is shivering from cold? In short, how can I live in luxury when my neighbor lacks the necessities?"

Jesus' example provides Stoll with a third reason for simple living. "When Jesus was here, he left us an outstanding example of simple living. . . . Not only did Jesus set a personal example to inspire us and guide us, he also gave us many teachings . . . [about] the danger of material possessions and the importance of trusting God on a daily basis for our food and clothing."

Finally, writes Stoll, forgoing a dishwasher provides work for his children, so they "have something to do." Doing dishes, he says, is "much better for their character than being idle, or expecting others to do things for them all the time." Plus, he notes, if his family bought a dishwasher, they'd need to get their house wired, and then "we might as well get all those other laborsaving appliances and devices . . . a vacuum cleaner, a dryer, a toaster, a blender, a microwave, and on and on." For all these reasons, "We say 'no thanks' to the dishwasher."[2]

Jesus, the Ordnung, and iPods

Many religious traditions make connections between spirituality and material possessions, but few make these connections as clearly or as frequently as the Amish. Would any of us, for example, consult a pastor, rabbi, or other spiritual leader before buying a BlackBerry or a flat-screen TV? From dishwashers to clothing, from televisions to tractors, Amish spirituality intersects with the material world at almost every turn.

Amish religion is not only broader in its reach but also more collective in its application. *Ordnung* guidelines on technology and other possessions supersede personal choice. Amish society is not a communal society in the sense of holding property in common (there is no community-owned property, not even church buildings), but the community does hold sway over what individuals may and may not own.

Jesus did not give advice on dishwashers, iPods, or DVDs, of course. As new technologies appear, Amish people observe their impact on people and communities in the larger society. Those that seem harmless—chain saws, gas barbecue grills, trampolines, for example—are accepted with little concern. Those that directly threaten religious values and family life, however, are discouraged, if not completely banned. "It is not that the plain people oppose all new ideas and practices," says an Amish author. "There is a need to choose only those that will be of genuine benefit, and to reject those that break down the values we uphold. This would apply to modern appliances and household gadgets, many of which have the potential to change our family and community-oriented way of life in ways we may not realize until the damage has been done."[3]

As we noted in Chapter Four, the *Ordnung* consists of the church's collective interpretation of issues the Bible doesn't directly address. The rules of the *Ordnung* pertaining to technology, dress, and lifestyle shape the Amish way of life. These understandings—whether to play musical instruments, wear neckties, install wall-to-wall carpeting, and so on—are Amish applications of biblical principles for daily living. Because the Amish believe that the Bible speaks directly to such issues as fraud, murder, divorce, and fornication, the *Ordnung* is not needed for them. Nor does the *Ordnung* address things the Amish consider obviously wrong, such as gambling, or clearly harmless, like eating pizza.

Some issues are not easily or quickly resolved. On contentious matters, such as telephones, which one grandmother claimed were "on probation" for several decades in her *Gmay*, decisions evolve slowly. Once a practice gels, however, it becomes wedded to religious tradition when the church ratifies the *Ordnung*. This endorsement makes the *Ordnung* rather resistant to change. Nonetheless, the *Ordnung* does flex, albeit slowly, and new convictions are grafted into it as needed.

Because the final say on the *Ordnung* rests with each *Gmay*, the dozens of different answers to the same question create a zigzag pattern of practices across Amish groups. The answers to the question of how to chill food, for example, range from using gas refrigerators to using iceboxes, depending on the community. These practices, passed on by oral tradition, become "the way of our people." An Amish leader sums it up like this: "Our everyday life cannot be separated from our religion."[4]

Enemy Territory

Amish people see life as a spiritual struggle. As baptismal candidates kneel and confess their faith in Christ, they renounce three things: their self, the devil, and the world. This trio threatens the spiritual well-being of the community: selfishness produces pride and disobedience, the cunning devil with his bag of tricks can lead members astray, and the lure of worldly things can pollute the purity of the church.

"The world," in the Amish mind, means the values and vices of the dominant society. The deep reservations the Amish have about the world did not begin with them or even with their sixteenth-century Anabaptist ancestors. They originated in the Bible, in texts that leaders often cite, including "Love not the world, neither the things that are in the world" (1 John 2:15), "Wherefore come out from among them, and be ye separate, saith the Lord" (2 Corinthians 6:17), and perhaps most important, the apostle Paul's admonition, "Be not conformed to this world, but be ye transformed by the renewing of your mind" (Romans 12:2).

Stoll, describing Christians as pilgrims on a journey to heaven, writes, "We are in enemy territory, and we dare not linger."[5] Not all Amish people would call the world "enemy territory," but most do believe that Satan is an active force for evil in the world. The worldliness of mass society is dangerous precisely because Satan controls it. "Rules of a Godly Life" describes Satan's cunning tactics to "ensnare" people and control them like a "fowler can hold a bird by one leg."[6]

Amish minister Ben Blank describes how Satan shapes popular culture through music. "Many [people] are filled from early morning to late night with the satanically inspired music of lust and greed," Blank writes. These sounds "saturate and keep good thinking out of our minds," which soon "become filled with this garbage, pushing out the good."[7] Separation from the world, according to the Amish way of thinking, means keeping a cautious distance from the evils of mass culture: violence, promiscuous sex, abortion, war, greed, fraud, divorce, excessive consumption, and so on.

This brings us back to possessions. In the Amish view, possessions and certain types of technology can harm the spiritual well-being of members by luring them into worldly practices. Although a particular possession may not be sinful in itself, an overriding desire for it may interfere with one's affections for God. Having the possession may also enable its owner to pursue other evils that wouldn't be possible to pursue otherwise.

Are Cars Immoral?

Although Amish people associate spiritual consequences with certain technological gadgets, they are not anti-technology, nor do they consider technological devices sinful. "A car is not immoral," a bishop told us, "it's what it will lead to that's the problem."

What do cars lead to? In a word: fragmentation. Explains one Amish writer, "[The car's] social effect on the American family has been profound, with members heading off in all directions and leading essentially separate lives." If the *Gmay* were to allow car ownership, "the structure of the community [would] change. Members of the same church may live ten, twenty or even fifty miles apart, attending church faithfully, and yet being totally unattached to the life of the community."[8] In contrast, horse-drawn transportation holds communities together by slowing the pace and limiting mobility.

Beyond splintering communities, the car, an icon of contemporary Western life, symbolizes speed, independence, status, and power—values that fly in the face of Amish aspirations for community, humility, and simplicity. Indeed, the most defining aspect of Amish identity is their rejection of the car. "It's the first thing people get when they leave the church," noted one member. "The automobile has claimed a prominent place in people's lives," said an Amish leader, "and men are known and judged by the automobiles they drive. Is it not expedient to remain apart from such a culture as much as possible?"

Because cars are not considered immoral in and of themselves, members often ride in them, hiring non-Amish owners of cars or vans to take them to funerals in faraway communities, on vacations, to out-of-town doctors, and for business travel at home. This use-but-don't-drive policy strikes some outsiders as hypocritical, but it reveals Amish assumptions about technology. First, major technological decisions rest in the hands of the church, not individuals. Second, because technology is not inherently evil, it can be used with caution. Third, keeping technology at arm's length is a continual reminder of the dangers lurking near it. In sum, technologies like the car aren't inherently sinful, but they do pose spiritual perils. In the face of such perils, the church's wisdom is the best defense.

Pulling the Plug

If, as the Amish claim, cars expose their owners to worldly perils, so too does the electric current pulsing through modern homes. Significantly, one of the chief Amish concerns about electricity echoes their concern about the car: fragmentation. "The unlimited use of electric current puts a world of power . . . at our fingertips that is not good for us," writes one Amish leader, because the conveniences it runs "tend to disperse the family throughout the house in the evenings instead of encouraging togetherness and communication." The Amish also know that electric current would likely bring an avalanche of household conveniences—computers, televisions, microwaves, and many other items—that would disrupt their lives. Because hooking up to the public grid would connect Amish people too directly to the outside world, very few of the eighteen hundred Amish congregations allow tapping electricity that way.

Even in the realm of electricity, however, the Amish are not absolute objectors. Many Amish people use batteries to power clocks, reading lights, hand-held tools, and, in some communities, such equipment as electric typewriters, copiers, and cash registers. LED lights are commonplace on some buggies and are used for many other purposes. Solar power—what some call "hooking up to God's grid"—is a growing source of electric power in certain areas.

Amish people also draw on nonelectric power sources. In some Amish homes, propane gas powers refrigerators, stoves, and heaters, as well as portable lights, though in more traditional communities, wood-fired cookstoves, iceboxes, and outhouses of early twentieth-century vintage are more typical. Hydraulic and pneumatic power, produced by diesel engines, operates equipment in some machine shops. In Amish communities that are more open to change, households may even use pneumatic power to operate such appliances as mixers, sewing machines, and washing machines.

But even with these alternate power sources, Amish homes are remarkably quiet; the silence is punctuated only by ticking clocks and family chatter. They have none of the modern noisemakers to which most of us have grown so accustomed—no dishwashers, microwaves, doorbells, vacuum cleaners, air conditioners, telephones, digital timers, or hair dryers. Amish homes also lack media technology; computers, radios, DVD players, and televisions are all forbidden. The Amish believe that resisting these technologies not only makes their lives quieter but also keeps them safe from moral peril.

One Amish writer, commenting on the evils of TV, claims that many television programs "portray a way of life and a set of values not fitting for the Christian. How many minds have been damaged and polluted by the diet of romance and violence from these media? Forsaking these is one of the first and most important steps for anyone seeking a fuller and more committed Christian life."

Amish schools, devoid of all devices except battery-operated wall clocks, send a clear message to children: we will not let technology dictate our lives. The latest technologies may make some tasks easier, and they may even be fun to use, but they carry a cost, both economic and spiritual. From an Amish perspective, streaming popular media directly into the home or school would be an assault on the community's spiritual well-being. Why, they wonder, should a people striving to live apart from the world welcome worldly values into their homes? By and large they remain unconvinced that the benefits of certain technologies outweigh the costs.

Escaping Fads and Fashions

A well-dressed churchgoer leaving a Christmas Eve service once told us, "I wish I were Amish this time of the year so I wouldn't have to spend so much time trying to match my clothing." This woman was surely joking, but she hit on something important: the Amish don't spend much time selecting outfits for church or any other occasion. The decision about what to wear has already been made.

Although Amish dress practices vary by community, each group has a standard wardrobe governed by its *Ordnung*. "These dress standards," explains one church leader, "are like a railing surrounding the balcony of a house to protect its occupants. . . . The individual Christian is not sufficient unto himself—he needs the church." Amish dress is thus one more demonstration of *uffgevva*, giving up the right to dress as one pleases and yielding to the community, which defines and enforces the moral order.[9]

"Who should decide what is proper, modest, and practical?" this leader asks. "Shall this be left up to the individual? The popular spirit declares 'my life is my own to live. No one has the right to tell me what to do or how to dress.'" In the Amish view the church has a responsibility to "set up guidelines and standards for its members to live by. As a brotherhood counseling together, the church decides what is safe and what is not safe, what is proper and what is not."

When asked why they follow certain practices, many Amish people reply, "That's just what our people do." Leaders, however, view dress practices as applications of values found in the New Testament: humility, modesty, separation, and self-denial. The Amish publication *1001 Questions and Answers on the Christian Life* has forty-three questions and answers on dress—second only to the topic of heaven, which merits fifty-eight questions.[10] One key New Testament verse on dress can be found in 1 Timothy 2:9, where the apostle Paul instructs women to adorn themselves in "modest apparel, . . . not with . . . gold, or pearls, or costly array." In another New Testament passage, women are warned against "outward adorning of plaiting the hair, and of wearing of gold, or of putting on of apparel." Rather, they should wear "the ornament of a meek and quiet spirit, which is in the sight of God of great price" (1 Peter 3:3–4). Amish leaders expect adult men to grow a beard, "because God created us that way" and because several verses in the Old Testament, such as Leviticus 19:27, mention the beard.

Although the details of *Ordnung* dress regulations vary from church to church, all Amish communities agree on two things. First, they forbid all jewelry, including wedding rings and wristwatches. Second, they require some form of plain garb. Regardless of its form, all clothing should be "neat, plain, simple, [and] serviceable," suggests one writer, and it should serve its purpose "in covering the body." Plain garb, he continues, is very different from worldly fashions, which are "made to give prominence to and advertise certain parts of the human form by means of extra padding, peculiar cuts, and thin fabrics which leave certain parts of the body exposed to the gaze of the public, . . . [cultivate] lust and pride . . . and give preference to the perverted tastes and erratic customs of a sinful world."

Amish deacon Paul Kline warns, "We dare not use dress to assert wealth, status or physical beauty in order to manipulate others for personal advantage." Church-regulated garb, he explains, "makes for a brotherhood. It is a way for individuals to express death to self-will."

Kline believes there is another positive side to church-prescribed clothing: "Uniform dress also provides an escape from the fashions of this world."[11] In the words of another leader, "The world is willing to make any sacrifice and pay any price to stay in fashion. They will paint their faces, pierce their ears, pluck their eyebrows, freeze their legs, and cramp their toes—none of which is comfortable, practical, sensible, or even beautiful."[12] Although it may look drab to outsiders, common garb eliminates lots of shopping and stress about keeping in style and looking good. Plain dress is a quiet way of resisting the changing fads and fashions of the modern world.

Seeking Simplicity

No cars, no televisions, no fancy dress—these aspects of Amish life, all of which point to their view of material possessions, are well known. But Amish spirituality shapes their approach to possessions in less obvious ways. With heaven as their home, they seek to have few earthly possessions and to hold them lightly. The way of *Gelassenheit*—of not striving to get ahead of others—"demands a plain and simple lifestyle. Our furnishings and way of life need to be plain and simple so as not to appear more wealthy than others," according to Deacon Kline.[13] "Unless we are truly humble, we are not truly plain," writes Sadie, a young mother. "We must be willing to be something less than our neighbor across the road."[14] For her, plainness stretches beyond simple dress and basic possessions to attitudes of humility and contentment.

Sadie sees holding possessions lightly as one of her responsibilities as a parent, for "eventually our children will see that the luxuries and complexities of the world are a hindrance to our faith." In addition to curbing her own desire to consume, however, she believes it's important for her—and other Amish parents—to rein in their children's desires. In an Amish family magazine, she offers these guidelines for teaching children simplicity: (1) keep toys few and simple; (2) dress and name dolls plainly; (3) teach basic sewing skills rather than embroidery and painting; (4) make new out of old in the course of hooking, braiding, and sewing rugs; (5) piece quilts from scraps of clothing; (6) remove needless fringes, ribbons, and tucks from dresses; and

133

(7) remind children "that the trend toward what is bigger, fancier, and more expensive leads rapidly in one direction—away from God."

Because these values have been handed down through the generations, Amish people have become experts at frugality, thrift, and practicality. Clothing is reused and passed on to others. Strips of old clothing are woven into braids for making rugs. Broken furniture and equipment is repaired, not tossed into the dumpster. From clothing to haircuts, goods and services are more likely to be home- or community-made than purchased at the mall. Amish businesspeople operate some fifty "bent-and-dent" stores that purchase surplus products from national chain stores. They clean and relabel canned and dry goods and sell them at discounts in these stores, which cater to both Amish and non-Amish customers.

Amish people uniformly praise the virtues of simplicity and plain living, but those ideals find many different expressions. Families in the most tradition-minded groups have austere homes without indoor plumbing, whereas others have spacious homes with fine cabinetry, exterior stone façades, and professional landscaping. Income level also varies, from that of small farmers who just make ends meet to that of owners of multimillion-dollar manufacturing firms. Despite this real economic diversity, the principles of simplicity and frugality minimize the signs of social class. All members wear similar garb, travel by horse and buggy, and will be buried in simple wooden coffins.

These practices are rooted in a spirituality that prizes humility above almost every other virtue. Those who show off their wealth or brag about it are charged with pride and arrogance, and those with traces of ostentatious living and conspicuous consumption are chided. Pride, whether it is revealed by boasting about personal achievement or showcasing wealth, is considered sin.

The Amish also display a practical frugality that stems from two things: the survival skills of their rural heritage, and their spiritual understanding that human beings are stewards of material things. They are caretakers of the possessions given to them by God. In a lengthy admonition, one leader writes, "These earthly goods are not really ours—they are loaned to us by God, and we are to be responsible stewards."[15]

The Lure of Walmart

To be sure, Amish people struggle with their consumerist desires, trying to balance earthly possessions with eternal ones. One Amish minister cautions members not to desire "something here in this life that we should wait to have in eternity. . . . When the money comes in fast, we are apt to worship the golden calf of money."[16] Preachers often remind members that "the love of money is the root of all evil" (1 Timothy 6:10), and that Jesus urged people to lay up their treasures in heaven, not on earth (Matthew 6:20).

These warnings wouldn't be needed, of course, if Amish folks had no material desires. Amish people do shop at Walmart, however, and they join Costco and Sam's Club if they are nearby. They buy books, go on vacations, and appreciate well-crafted furniture. Amish hunters purchase state-of-the-art archery equipment, rifles, and camping gear. New buggies are a source of satisfaction, and you wouldn't be a true Amish man if you didn't find pleasure in a horse that's both spry and dependable. For their part, Amish children appreciate new skates, new scooters, and new baseball bats.

All things considered, however, the Amish are surely less possessed by earthly possessions than most Americans. Their rejection of fashionable dress, motor vehicles, public-grid electricity, television, and other electronic media provides formidable resistance in an all-consuming world that often equates happiness with the purchase of material things.

Living in a mostly media-free zone, they are sheltered from the seductive blitz of Madison Avenue ads that punctuate television shows and pop up on computer screens.

As pilgrims on a path to heaven that meanders through a world of things, Amish people struggle with temptations as they try to keep their eyes on the heavenly prize. But those temptations hold less sway in a community that continually reminds its members that this world is not their home. Simplicity is "not the key to eternal life," writes Sadie, the young Amish mother. "Yet we feel plainness is necessary evidence that we have set our affection on things eternal."[17]

CHAPTER TEN

Nature

All children should have a creek wandering through their childhood.

—AMISH BISHOP

It was a sultry August Sunday in Ohio. An elderly bishop in Stark County had invited us to a church service in a member's barn where newly threshed oats overflowed the granaries. As we arrived, the women gathered in the farmhouse, while the men formed an oval under the barn's forebay. We joined the men in conversation as little boys in bare feet milled about. As more carriages arrived, a hostler brought each horse into the barn, breaking our circle as he passed through it. The sound of horses snorting and munching grain, the pungent smell of manure, and the constant buzz of bees and flies offered a prelude for the service.

The barn's second floor served as the sanctuary. Backless wooden benches formed twenty-foot rows—four rows on the left facing five rows on the right, with an aisle down the middle. The men filled the left-hand rows, with a large mound of straw behind them. Fresh-cut timothy hay overflowed the storage mow behind the women.

The morning was hot and humid, and it only grew hotter as the three-hour service wore on. Pigeons cooed from the rafters and fluttered between the mows. Horses neighed in the stalls below us, and tiny oat ticks hopped around on the floor. The large, open barn doors offered a view of rolling fields of tall green corn, brownish oat stubble, and a distant ridge of trees.

Whether a *Gmay* meets in a home, barn, or shop, Amish worship bumps up against the natural world in many ways. The lack of air conditioning, electric lights, and automated heating means that Amish worshipers are attuned to nature's elements every time they meet—though some times more than others. One member recalls a preacher halting his sermon for fifteen minutes while waiting for a noisy thunderstorm to pass. On another occasion, worship ended abruptly when cows broke through a fence and the men rushed out to herd them back. From thunderclaps to barking dogs, from insect-laden flypaper to stifling heat, nature is never far away.

This connection to nature is rooted in the rural lifestyle of the Amish. Although many Amish today no longer farm, all continue to live in rural areas. A few reside in small villages or on the outskirts of towns, but none live in cities. In fact, most Amish people hold a strong bias against city life. One writer declares that in Genesis 4, after Cain murdered his brother Abel, he fled from God and built a city, "which he peopled with his wicked descendants . . . [and] cities have been degenerating ever since." The country, in contrast, offers rich possibilities for communion with God, the writer continues. "Life in the country is awake to the natural order of daylight and dark, sunshine and rain, the swing of the seasons, and the blessings with which God has ordered our world." All of this, he concludes, is much better than an "artificial environment of urban centers where night is well-lit, rain is the way to ruin a day, and food and fiber originate at the local store."[1]

A Window into Heaven

Although Amish spirituality is closely tied to an experience of the natural world, the Amish believe that God transcends nature. In the words of the Dordrecht Confession, God created "all things visible and invisible," which he still "governs and upholds . . . by his wisdom, might, and the word of his power."[2] Unlike traditional Native American religions, Amish spirituality does not see supernatural forces embedded in nature, such as spirits in the trees or ancestral voices in the winds. Still, because the Amish view the created world as God's handiwork, it serves an important spiritual function, drawing them closer to God and teaching them about God's power and providential care. "God's beautiful and marvelous creation," writes one minister, "is like looking through a small window into Heaven, especially when we think of His beauty, truth, and love."[3]

The Amish way rests on prescientific assumptions about the natural world. Amish people affirm a literal reading of the creation account in Genesis 1 and 2. Evolution is considered heresy. One writer describes evolutionary theory as "an attempt to explain life without bringing God into the picture." While admitting that the biblical account "leaves some questions unanswered," he considers anything other than a literal six-day creation to be "wisdom of this world" that is "foolishness with God" (1 Corinthians 3:19).[4] Another writer concurs: "The only way for us to learn how this interesting universe had its beginning would be for God to tell us about it. And He has done exactly this, very plainly, in the first chapter of the Bible."[5]

Although framed by the Bible, Amish views on nature draw from other sources as well. Many of the six-thousand-plus church leaders own copies of *Raber's Almanac*, which is published by an Amish bookstore in Ohio and distributed nationwide. Updated each year, this one-hundred-page booklet includes the lectionary of scripture readings for church services, a directory of church districts, and the names of church leaders across the country.

But *Raber's Almanac* also brims with information about nature. The inside cover shows solar and lunar eclipses for the year, zodiac signs, and the dates when Mercury and Venus are visible in the morning and evening sky. Each month has its own page in the almanac. The front side of the page features the phases of the moon, the lectionary scriptures for each Sunday in that month, and selected Bible verses, poetry, or hymns. A chart on the back side of the page shows solar and lunar details and the astrological symbol for each day of that month.

The content of *Raber's Almanac* blends rural folk culture with a biblical worldview. "More Amish than will admit it still plant some of their seeds according to certain astrological signs," one bishop says. "My father would sow the spring clover in the sign of Leo in March. Some neighbors plant potatoes on or the day after the May full moon, radishes at a waning moon, and above-ground crops in a waxing moon."[6] The bishop adds that many aspects of Amish life, such as the hymns sung in church, follow seasonal patterns. "In the spring we sing of the skylark trilling its love song and then in autumn of the coming cold season."

Even more than the seasons, daily weather occupies a central place in Amish life, in conversations, letter-writing, and even sermons. Whether looking at the stars, tracking migratory birds, or talking about hail and rain, people are attuned to nature's impulses and find in them compelling evidence of God's power and majesty.

Out in the Fields with God

This enduring belief in the goodness of God's creation is one reason why farming plays such an important role in Amish life. Even though many families have left the farm, pushed off by rising land prices or lured by other jobs, farm life remains the ideal. In the words of one person, farming "allows us to be part of the cycle of life, death, and renewal that God planned in His wisdom. In our daily contact with creation we cannot help but stand in awe and wonder of God."[7] In his organic farming column in the Amish publication *The Diary*, Moses Esh recalls a poem he learned in school, titled "Out in the Fields with God."

> The little cares that fretted me
> I lost them yesterday
> Among the fields above the sea
> Among the winds at play;
>
> . . . .
>
> Among the husking of the corn,
> Where drowsy posies nod,
> Where ill thoughts die and good are born
> Out in the fields with God.[8]

Surely this sentiment—standing near to God in a field of grain—describes the experience of many non-Amish farmers too, but the feeling likely runs deeper among the Amish because they farm with horses. One farmer explains, "When I am cultivating corn on a 75-degree, late June day with a team [of horses] that responds perfectly to my voice, and I listen to the cheerful flight songs of the bobolinks in the hayfield nearby, I think we farmers must be the most fortunate people on earth."[9] Farming with horses is not easy work, of course, and this farmer might sing a different tune on a 90-degree day when the flies are biting and his draft horses are acting up. Still, unlike sitting in the air-conditioned cab of a noisy diesel tractor, farming with horses offers close contact with the soil, a full measure of fresh air, and the endless chatter of birds. "I often joke," says one Amish writer, "that if tractors can plow a six-acre field in two hours, I figure on two days, but my time includes listening to vesper sparrows and meadow larks and watching clouds scud across the sky."[10]

It's not just farmers who revel in nature: Amish people who have left the farm or never farmed at all also find inspiration in the outdoors. On an acre or two of land, they raise gardens, care for horses, and let their windows open to the breezes, smells, and sounds of nature. With few entertainments to keep them indoors—no Internet, no cable television, and no video game systems—nonfarm families frequently spend time in nature.

Virtually all Amish families, those that farm and those that don't, have gardens that supply them with fresh or canned vegetables year-round. Families also buy many groceries in stores, but nearly all households produce a large share of the food they eat. Underscoring the benefits of growing her own food, one grandmother notes that "good, wholesome food" makes the family meal "a sacred ritual." "If we know where everything on the table comes from," she writes, it "seems to make us more aware and thankful to God."[11]

Tending vegetable or flower gardens is time-consuming and physically taxing, for it entails an endless struggle with weeds, bugs, mildew, and drought. Still, like the hay fields of the farmers, gardens are a place of spiritual nourishment as well as labor. One Amish woman described her experience in her flower garden:

> I am strolling through my garden
> in the early morning dew.
> And I fill myself with happiness
> to last the whole day through.
> I talk to yellow butter cups
> they seem to understand
> The poppies nod their dainty heads
> just like a little band.[12]

Creeks and Children

In his book *Last Child in the Woods: Saving Our Children from Nature-Deficit Disorder*, journalist Richard Louv worries that "over-scheduled, over-organized" twenty-first-century children are being harmed by their detachment from nature. He recommends one hundred activities for parents to remedy their children's nature-deficit disorder, from digging in the dirt to walking under a full moon. The outdoors nurtures physical health and psychological wholeness, Louv says, and even contributes to children's spiritual well-being.

Louv need not worry about Amish children. Immersed in nature from birth, they spend much of their early years digging in the dirt and chasing wild things. Toddlers follow their older siblings and parents around as they work in the garden and tend animals. In addition to having pets, many children are responsible for caring for chickens, calves, cats, and dogs at an early age. Amish children don't play sports in organized athletic leagues, so their outdoor experiences are not tied to the "manicured playing fields" that, according to Louv, have replaced nature-oriented parks and play spaces in the lives of most American children.[13]

Family activities often revolve around nature, sometimes combining work and recreation. Some families, for instance, enjoy picking wild fruits and berries, often along fence rows that provide shelter for creatures that children find intriguing. Amish bishop David Kline is a farmer, naturalist, and author, whose books are widely read by outsiders. He describes a springtime walk when he took his youngest daughter to a nearby creek in search of hidden treasures. "The winter winds created new sand and gravel bars, and we loved to comb those deposits for Indian artifacts [and] old bottles," he writes. But in addition to finding human artifacts, Kline and his daughter found evidence of God's creative work—the tracks of minks, raccoons, muskrat, and even freshwater mussels. His conclusion from that experience echoes Louv's ideas about what benefits children: "All children should have a creek winding through their childhood."[14]

This bond with nature is nurtured by the literature children read. Many Amish publications include a children's section with nature-related poems, stories, and crossword puzzles. *Family Life* magazine has a "Pre-School Corner" with simple exercises that challenge children to separate farm animals from wild ones or match animal mothers with their babies. Textbooks in Amish schools, devoid of current events, feature wildlife stories that introduce students to the plant and animal kingdoms. This is even true of math books. One sixth-grade math book includes three nature-related units: "On the Farm," "Insects," and "The Greenhouse." One problem in the insect unit poses this question: "Steve found 16 crickets. If half of them each laid 295 tiny banana-shaped eggs, how many cricket eggs were there?"[15]

Wild Things and "Honey Spots"

The Lost Creek Shoe Shop in Mifflintown, Pennsylvania, an Amish-owned and -operated store, is known at least as well for its binoculars as for its shoes. Make your way through the strong smell of leather in the front room, past the shelves of hiking boots and work shoes, and you'll find a back room overflowing with optical devices—from beginner binoculars for less than a hundred dollars to state-of-the-art spotting scopes that will run you several thousand. Step outside to the observation deck, and you can try them out on the warblers and blue-birds that inhabit creek banks and wooded areas around the store.

Because their childhoods are steeped in nature, it's not surprising that Amish adults find spiritual refreshment and renewal in such hobbies as bird watching. A column devoted to birding appears monthly in

The Diary, and families travel by van or bus to migratory sites. For some, birding is an intergenerational hobby. A few years ago we participated in an Audubon Society–sponsored Christmas bird count led by an Amish man who roused us—and his elementary school–age grandsons—at 5:00 A.M. to "call in" owls.

Amish people enjoy many outdoor forms of recreation. Those living near the Chesapeake Bay, the Atlantic Ocean, or inland lakes frequently fish as well as hunt for ducks or geese. Although many *Gmay*s forbid members from owning motor boats, some fishermen rent them. In some communities, unbaptized teens, unconstrained by the *Ordnung*, enjoy waterskiing on rivers and lakes.

Killing humans is considered a sin, but the Amish have few qualms about shooting animals. Hunting, especially for deer, is widespread in Amish communities from Maryland to Montana. Those who hunt consider it a mix of recreation and work, noting that they are harvesting meat and sometimes protecting their gardens and crops.

Another common recreational activity is stargazing. Several Amish publications have monthly columns on sky watching, with suggestions for finding stars and tracking planets and their moons. A September column advised, "In the morning Venus rises in a dark sky a little north of east. Mars is high in the east and right of Venus. By October 1, look low in the east for dim Saturn, brighter Mercury a little higher, and gleaming Venus above the pair." A Bible passage that appears in some sky-watching columns reminds readers of the grandeur of God's creation: "When I consider thy heavens, the work of thy fingers, the moon and the stars, which thou hast ordained; What is man, that thou art mindful of him?" (Psalm 8:3–4).[16]

Birds and stars are favorites, but Amish appreciation for the natural world is wide ranging. David Kline recounts a walk he took on a forty-five-acre plot of land that one of his friends called "a small honey spot." Kline was inspired by what he found: "The wind in the trees and

145

the water flowing over the shale-bottom creek seemed to whisper, do not come closer. Take off your gum boots, because you are standing on holy ground. . . . The sight of the hepaticas in bloom reaffirmed my belief that many of us need wild, unspoiled places where we feel close to God."[17]

In some ways, Kline's ramble on the "honey spot" is unusual, for it appears he hiked there by himself. It's more typical for Amish people to enjoy the gifts of nature with others. Whether birding, fishing, or collecting berries, the Amish usually do things in groups, visiting and chatting as they go. Their recreational practices reveal their appreciation for the outdoors and their commitment to collective, participatory activities. Although some youth and adults occasionally buy tickets to sporting events, the bulk of Amish recreation involves do-it-yourself activities, such as hiking and birding, rather than spectator ones.

Are We Good Shepherds?

The Amish know that the natural world contains more than pretty birds to watch and "honey spots" for hikers. They also know nature's raw, violent side firsthand. Children see red-tailed hawks snatching up mice, and foxes eating chickens. They see bulls mating with cows, wet chicks hatching, and slimy calves slipping from their mothers' wombs. They see dogs dying, worms infesting broccoli, and blood dripping from the necks of roosters that lost their heads on the chopping block. They see cows shaded by an oak tree in the pasture, only to be seared by lightning a few hours later as they huddle under its branches for shelter. Theirs is often a grubby and gruesome encounter with the natural world.

These everyday observations in gardens, barnyards, and fields also mean that the Amish, unlike many North Americans, know where their food comes from. They see the direct link between the milk on their cereal and the cow, the baked potato and the garden, the fried chicken leg and the bird that used to perch on it. Their view of nature is unsanitized and unsentimental. Death is seen as a natural part of life, not something that happens in a faraway slaughterhouse or even in a local veterinary hospital where pets are "put to sleep."

When deciding how to deal with the natural world, the Amish take their cues from both their farm-based heritage and from Genesis 1:26, where God gives the first humans "dominion over the fish of the sea, and over the fowl of the air, and over the cattle, and over all the earth." The Amish believe, as do many Christians, that this God-given assignment means that humans have both the ability and the obligation to manage nature—farming its fields, mining its resources, and domesticating its animals.

The specifics of this human dominion—what is acceptable behavior and what is not—are often a source of contention, among Christians and sometimes among the Amish as well. Some Amish farmers treat their cows like milk machines, work their horses too long without water, and raise pet-store-bound puppies in cramped kennels. For them, dominion means squeezing benefits from animals with the least amount of cost. Like some Christians in the broader world who treat the natural world as their slave, these Amish farmers regard nature as little more than a means to an economic end.

Other Amish people take a different approach. An article in *Family Life* reminds readers that "the animals that share the earth with us are flesh and blood like we are. They have feelings of thirst and hunger, tiredness and pain just like we have. . . . Our domestic animals are willing servants when they are treated kindly and with respect."[18] David Kline's deep affection for his "voice-activated horses" derives in part from the horse's role in Amish life, which goes far beyond pulling a plow. "The horse is our pacer," says Kline. "He sets our pace of living. When he needs to stop at lunch, we take a break. If we need to rest him in the afternoon, it gives us a natural break in the flow of things. We can't use horses for night work, and so it gives us a break in the evening."[19]

When expressing his love for animals, Kline often cites *Christenpflicht*, the Amish prayer book. He's especially fond of a friend's translation of this line at the end of a five-page prayer: "and help us be gentle with your creatures and handiwork so that we may abide in your eternal salvation and continue to be held in the hollow of your hand."[20]

For Bishop Kline, these words signal a mutually dependent relationship with nature, "whether with the robins in the dooryard, the domestic animals, the dog by the wood stove or herding sheep, even the earthworms." He then continues, "The question we need to ask ourselves is: are we good shepherds to these animals entrusted to our care? . . . The only way we can repay the animals in our care is with kindness."[21]

Few Amish people articulate the connections between nature and Amish spirituality as clearly as Kline. But others have espoused similar ideas. Writing in the 1970s, one Amish leader noted, "After a man becomes a Christian, his animals will feel the difference." For this man, Jesus' words, "Blessed are the merciful, for they shall obtain mercy," directed Amish farmers to be mindful of their animals' feelings of "pain, thirst, and hunger."[22] For his part, Kline traces his views to his Amish father. "My dad always considered it his duty, especially in the wintertime, to provide for the animals in his care—good feed, fresh water, and a clean and dry place to sleep—before returning to the house for his own meal. He always thought, or at least I got the impression, that how we treated the animals is how he expected to be treated by God. A simple practice of the Golden Rule: treat the lives in our care with respect, love, and compassion."[23]

"Green Amish"

An Amish friend occasionally e-mails us from a computer in a non-Amish company where he works. He calls some of his friends—the ones engaged in organic farming, solar power, and recycling projects—"Green Amish." "Hey, maybe I could drive these Green Amish up to your place in my solar-powered electric buggy," he joked in one e-mail. "It has an auxiliary engine powered by fuel made in an anaerobic manure digester which we feed with a potent cow manure produced by an eco-friendly diet of organic baked beans."

Not many of our Amish friends send us e-mail messages. And not all Amish are green, although some are moving in that direction. Most Amish farmers, in tandem with other American farmers, started using chemical fertilizers, pesticides, and herbicides in the mid-twentieth century. More recently, however, some have begun to raise organic vegetables and poultry. With the help of outside expertise, Green Field Farms, a well-known Amish cooperative based in Ohio, and other Amish farms and businesses now sell organic products in national markets. Other Amish farmers have started dairies that produce milk from grass-fed cows, and farms that sell grass-fed beef.

This move to organic and other sustainable farming practices reflects Amish attentiveness to a growing consumer market for natural, organic foods. But it also emerges from deep springs in Amish spirituality, which has long emphasized the goodness of God's creation and humanity's responsibility to care for it. In a how-to booklet, fifteen Amish farmers describe their motivation for grass-based farming: "We, in the spirit of good land stewardship, are managers of the primary plant of God's creation—grass. We harvest this grass in the most ecological way by our cooperation with the laws of nature and the dictates of the bovine species. We then sell her milk as a reward for our

149

stewardship and gain the satisfaction of providing our families and our communities in a manner that violates neither the earth nor those that tread upon it."[24]

David Kline was green long before it became trendy. He summarizes his theology for eco-friendly living in these words: "If one's livelihood comes from the earth—from the land, from creation on a sensible scale, where humans are a part of the unfolding of the seasons, experience the blessings of drought-ending rains, and seek God's spirit in all creation—a theology for living should be as natural as the rainbow following a summer storm. And then we can pray, 'Help us to walk gently on the earth and to love and nurture your creation and handiwork.'"[25]

If his people remember this, Kline is sure they will be living the Amish way, the way described by another bishop in these words: "We should live as if Jesus would return today, and . . . take care of the land as if he would not be coming for one thousand years."

CHAPTER ELEVEN

Evil

We don't believe in pressing charges or going to court.

—AMISH MAN *whose relative was killed by a negligent driver*

Amo-bashing," the assailants called it. In 1996 near the northern Indiana towns of Bremen and Nappanee, five men and one woman targeted Amish men riding bicycles along country roads. Pulling their car alongside a cyclist, one person would lean out the window, brandish a tire iron, and club the Amish rider on the back or the head. They would then rob the man of his wallet and speed off.

As many as fifteen Amish victims suffered this fate—but responded with silence. Even though some had suffered head injuries or broken collarbones, they refused to report the attacks to the police. Finally, however, one of the men, Earl Slabaugh, decided to report a description of the car when its occupants narrowly missed hitting him. "He didn't run to the cops to get [the assailants] in trouble," Slabaugh's wife explained when reporters sought the family's comment. He did it because he feared someone would eventually die.

Meanwhile, the Kosciusko County deputy prosecutor was frustrated with "the reluctance of the Amish community to come forward, report incidents and testify against someone." This silence, said the prosecutor, made his task "extremely difficult." He was irritated because he knew it would be "nearly impossible to impeach an Amish witness, whose reputation for truth and credibility precede him by generations."

The Amish had different priorities. After police arrested the assailants, Slabaugh went to the restaurant where the driver of the car worked. He told the young woman that he forgave her and hoped she would stop before she became involved in more serious crimes. "We have to forgive them," a member of Slabaugh's *Gmay* explained. "We just can't forget it. We have to remember it for our own benefit, to teach our younger generation to stay out of things like that." Offering words that were sure to baffle the prosecutor, the church member agreed that the police and court system had to stop wrongdoers. But he refused to comment on the assailants' jail sentences. "That's too close to judging," he said.[1]

The Amish response to evil and wrongdoing strikes many outsiders as contradictory, if not hypocritical. Yet few things highlight more poignantly the beliefs and practices that stand at the center of their spirituality.

The Problem of Evil

Evil is a conundrum that every spiritual tradition faces. Is evil real or illusory? Is it produced by humans, supernatural forces, or a blend of both? Can evil be overcome, and if so, how? Drawing on the biblical text, the Amish have a clear sense that the world is not as God intended it to be, and they trace the roots of evil to the sin of rebellion. They see evil personified in the devil, or Satan, who rebelled against God and was cast out of heaven before the creation of the world. Later, the devil tempted the first humans, Adam and Eve, to doubt God's authority and become their own masters. As a result of their disobedience, Adam and Eve had to leave the perfect Garden of Eden, and life on earth has been plagued by sin ever since.

The Amish see evil as affecting everyone's life, and they do not believe they are immune from sin or the suffering sin causes. Nor do they think that they can achieve moral perfection. Amish writing, soaked in the language of humility, accents human shortcomings and the need for divine pardon. "Is there an escape route [from evil]?" asks one Amish writer. "Yes, through Jesus Christ, repentance, and grace through faith."[2] As we observed in Chapter Six, the *Gmay* and its rituals of confession and restoration offer an antidote to personal sin and a salve for its harmful effects.

When faced with wrongdoing at the hands of others, the Amish believe they should not resist evil with evil. Their understanding of nonresistance comes from Jesus' Sermon on the Mount: "Ye have heard that it hath been said, An eye for an eye, and a tooth for a tooth: But I say unto you, That ye *resist not evil*: but whosoever shall smite thee on thy right cheek, turn to him the other also. . . . Love your enemies, bless them that curse you, do good to them that hate you, and pray for them which despitefully use you, and persecute you" (Matthew 5:38–39, 44, emphasis added). This text, in which Jesus calls his followers to return good for evil, grounds Amish pacifism, their refusal to litigate, and their rejection of self-defense.

"When we consider the example of Christ, we see that He expressed no revenge against his enemies," insisted David Beiler, a nineteenth-century Amish bishop whose writings continue to carry great weight. Beiler was not bothered in the least by Bible stories that portray people engaged in warfare, seemingly with God's blessing, since Christ's example trumps everything. To Beiler, the scriptures made clear that Jesus "preferred to avoid confrontation, and He did not drag those who injured Him before a worldly court."[3] In similarly sharp language, the Dordrecht Confession declares, "Christ forbade and ruled out all revenge and retaliation."[4]

This theme of nonresistance appears frequently in children's stories and school texts, often taking aim at what the Amish see as the natural aggression of men and boys. In one popular series of Amish-authored books, a boy named Benjie is teased by a boy named Enos. Benjie's older brother tells him that "it takes a real man to stand up to mockery. Anyone can tease and mock, but not everyone can take it without fighting back. I know it's hard to return good for evil, but God will help you." Benjie resolved to "just smile and think, 'you can tease me all you want, Enos, but I will still love you.'"[5]

The Amish response to evil entails a combination of silence, patience, and forgiveness. This response is grounded in their under-standing of God's providence.

Thy Will Be Done

Providence, the idea that God "unceasingly cares for the world, that all things are in God's hands, and that God is leading the world to its appointed goal," is a central affirmation of Christianity.[6] How to mesh such a conviction with the reality of evil has long been a source of debate among Christians. Some resolve the dilemma by believing that God grants humans free will and does not stop them from acting on evil desires. Others hold that God sometimes allows evil things to happen for purposes that are not immediately obvious but are part of some greater long-term good in God's big-picture plan. Still others argue that humans will never fully understand why bad things happen under God's watch.

The Amish answer to the problem of evil is neither airtight nor entirely consistent from one person to the next. In our conversations with Amish people, they offered all three of the aforementioned answers. Nonetheless, their unwavering confidence in God's providence inclines them toward the last two, leaving many questions unresolved. In the wake of the Nickel Mines tragedy, one Amish man told us, "I like to say a religion without mystery is like a wagon without wheels."

This does not mean that Amish people passively accept without question whatever happens. They freely admit to struggling with questions, doubts, and injustice. In a story recounting an array of hardships in his life, an Ohio Amish man named John A. N. Troyer reported that forty years later he still couldn't forget the evening when "a young boy in a car hit our buggy," killing Troyer's wife and son. "The days ahead looked dark to me," Troyer recalled. Then, less than a year later, he had an accident at work and had to have his arm amputated at the shoulder. "I often wondered, 'Why me?'"

Still, Troyer expresses typical Amish confidence that, despite his inability to understand why these things had happened, God understood. "Since we pray the Lord's Prayer every day, and say 'Thy will be done,' we want to accept the way it is."[7]

"Thy will be done" is one of the most common refrains in Amish life. Amish people submit themselves to God's will, believing that the divine will is sometimes clear and sometimes impossible to discern. For example, a minister preaching a funeral sermon for one of the victims of the Amish school shooting said that it is not God's will that people shoot one another, and in the same sermon suggested that the schoolgirls' deaths were somehow part of God's plan in a sense that humans might never fully understand.

In some cases, people find positive ways of understanding their pain without claiming to know any ultimate purpose behind it. Ada Borkholder, an Indiana Amish woman who contracted polio as a very young child writes, "I have often said if I had to have polio, then I am glad it was when I was young so I don't remember being active." She does not romanticize her suffering or claim that her condition served some greater good. She simply concludes, "Lord, Thy will be done."[8]

The Sound of Silence

Imagine a trial in which the defendants have decided to represent themselves. Imagine, then, that when it comes time for them to speak, they sit quietly, saying nothing at all. Nothing. They simply wait for the verdict.

The Amish commitment to silence as an expression of their belief in God's providence sometimes takes such a form. Through the years, Amish parents charged with not sending their children to high school and young men facing draft boards often asked to speak in their own defense—and then offered no defense at all, only silence. In the late 1970s, when school authorities in Nebraska challenged the legitimacy of Amish schooling, the Amish in one area quietly moved away, citing the words of Jesus that those who are persecuted in one place should move on rather than fight (Matthew 10:23).

Silence exemplifies *Gelassenheit*—a person's willingness to accept things without demanding an answer to why they happened the way they did. But silence is also an expression of nonresistance in a world that urges individuals to make themselves heard, a world in which political interest groups clamor to be the loudest voice in national debates. In contrast, the Amish note that Jesus mostly responded with silence when the Roman governor Pilate questioned him prior to his crucifixion (Matthew 27:11–14).

Silence in Amish life "is an active force, not a sign of introspection," observes anthropologist John A. Hostetler in his book

Amish Society. "There is the silence of pacifism, of turning the other cheek, which reaches back to the martyrs and to Christ himself. . . . When confused by a bureaucrat, outwitted by a regulation, or cursed by an outsider, the Amish person answers with silence." Ultimately, silence is "a way of living and forgiving, a way of embracing the community with charity and the offender with affection."[9]

This same disposition lies at the root of Amish refusal to participate in labor unions, which they see as coercive and demanding. "It is true that labor unions came into being because employers abused their authority," explains an Amish guidebook, and "labor unions, by giving a voice . . . to employees, served to correct this injustice." But a combative voice is not one the Amish want speaking for them. Instead, the church urges silence in the face of injustice: "We need to be willing to suffer."[10]

That is not to say that Amish people have no sense of justice. In the aforementioned children's story about Benjie, the author conveys the character's honest feelings when he finds himself the butt of Enos's jokes: "Now Benjie was very angry. . . . More than anything else, he wanted to knock Enos down and sit on him. He wanted to shake Enos until his teeth rattled."[11] The Amish way, however, is to turn such concerns for fairness and justice away from noisy protests and loud calls for revenge and toward the divine command to forgive.

Forgiving to Be Forgiven

A week before the Amish school shooting in Nickel Mines, a twelve-year-old Amish boy in the same area was killed in a hit-and-run accident.[12] He had been riding his scooter on the way to help his neighbors milk their cows when a pickup truck struck him, hit a fence post, and sped away. A newspaper reporter visited the boy's family the next day, and his mother conveyed a message to the driver of the truck: "She should come here. We would like to see her. We hold nothing against her." When the driver read the mother's words in the newspaper article, she went to visit the family and received their words of forgiveness. Over the next several weeks, she visited the family three more times.

Such a forgiving response is bewildering to most outsiders. Yet when the larger world expressed surprise at the grace extended after the school shooting, the Amish were surprised in return, wondering why people were making such a fuss over the act of forgiveness. Although Amish people understand that forgiveness is often difficult, they do not view it as unnatural or strange. As a practice of *uffgevva*, it fits comfortably within the wider pattern of Amish life. It does, however, place the Amish in bold contrast to many outsiders who see giving up *any* rights, including a justified right to anger or revenge, as abnormal.

As with so many other aspects of their lives, the Amish understand forgiveness to be a form of giving up—giving up bitterness and the right to revenge and replacing them with loving feelings and even acts of compassion toward the offender. Interviews with Amish people who have suffered grievous wrongs reveal that they are hardly sentimental about forgiveness. They understand that the process is often difficult and note that Jesus said that even minor infractions must be forgiven "seventy times seven," implying that forgiveness takes time and is often marked by failures along the way.

Yet they have no doubt that forgiving is the right thing to do. In fact, they are so certain of its necessity that they can state their commitment to forgive even before they fully feel that way, offering compassionate words and actions with confidence that loving emotions will follow. "Forgiveness stretches out over time," said one mother. "But you have to start out with the will to forgive. But the bitterness may reenter your mind from time to time, and then you have to think about forgiveness again."

With characteristic humility, Amish people can recount stories of failed forgiveness and grudges that have plagued an individual or family for years. But such accounts are stark reminders of how destructive bitterness can be, and reinforce the necessity of forgiveness for the forgiver's own well-being. Speaking from experience, one man explained that "the acid of hate destroys the container that holds it." An Amish minister, writing in the magazine *Family Life*, says, "The stress and wear and tear of bottling up a grudge can be hard on both mind and body," and "we are hurting nobody more than we are hurting ourselves if we don't keep our forgiving up to date." He concludes, "God has good reason for telling us not to let the sun go down upon our wrath. . . . we are to wipe our slates clean of all unforgiving grudges toward others every day."[13]

At the crux of it, Amish people are convinced that forgiving is the way to respond to evil because Jesus commanded it. Time and again, they point to the Lord's Prayer and its words about forgiveness, "Forgive us our debts as we forgive our debtors" (Matthew 6:12), as the reason to forgive. They point out that forgiveness is the only part of the prayer that Jesus underscores, telling his disciples, "For if ye forgive men their trespasses, your heavenly Father will also forgive you; but if ye forgive not men their trespasses, neither will your Father forgive your trespasses" (Matthew 6:14–15).

Theologians in other Christian traditions may debate the interpretation of these words, but to the Amish, the meaning is clear. "In order for God to forgive us, we must forgive our fellow men," the *Family Life* writer asserts. "If we do choose to be cold and unforgiving to others we should omit part of the familiar Lord's Prayer when we pray, because we are really asking God to grant us the same unforgiveness we are giving others. We are not worthy of God's forgiveness if we don't forgive others!"

Forgiving in order to be forgiven may strike some Christians as an ungracious attempt to manipulate God. The Amish do not see it that way. Instead, as with their understanding of salvation, they view their relationships with God and with others as so intertwined that it is impossible to pull them apart. "God wants us to forgive," explained one minister. "Anything he asks us to do, He will also help us to do. We are to pass on to others the same kind of love we daily receive from God."

The Amish also distinguish forgiveness from pardon, the act of releasing an offender from the penalties of his or her action. When a church member repeatedly breaks his or her baptismal commitment, other church members seek to forgive the person, but until the offender repents, the shame of shunning remains. In the case of criminal behavior—such as the case of "Amo-bashing" in Northern Indiana—the Amish expect that the judicial system will mete out punishment even as Amish victims nurture forgiveness and reach out to the wrongdoer in compassion.

Kicking the Problem Upstairs

Critics dismiss the Amish response to evil as irresponsible. The Amish, they say, simply "kick the problem upstairs," outsourcing justice to God. This absolves them of the duty to make moral judgments. The Amish do not object to this line of critique. In fact, they see this sort of moral division of labor as biblical. The Christian's responsibility is to forgive, they say, whereas justice lies in God's hands. Humans are simply not in a position to second-guess God's judgment. The Amish view of justice thus expresses their deep-seated patience. They do not feel an obligation to make history turn out right, but are satisfied to wait—and sometimes even suffer—in the meantime.

Amish writers frequently cite the Bible passage that calls Christians to leave revenge in God's hands: "Dearly beloved, avenge not yourselves . . . for it is written, Vengeance is mine; I will repay, saith the Lord." Instead, "if thine enemy hunger, feed him; if he thirst, give him drink" (Romans 12:19–20a). The Amish aversion to passing judgment also surfaces in their attitude toward other Christians. Amish people reject many aspects of contemporary culture, but unlike some exclusive sects, they expect to find many other Christians in heaven. When asked about the salvation of non-Amish Christians, they are quick to repeat these words of Jesus: "Judge not, that ye be not judged" (Matthew 7:1). Amish are loath to declare that non-Amish people are headed for hell, because only God knows their hearts and can rightly judge their faithfulness.

Similarly, the Amish refuse to condemn government completely. The Dordrecht Confession paints government as part of the fallen world from which Christians should separate themselves, and following early Anabaptist teachings, the Amish consider the government's use of violence un-Christian. Yet the Dordrecht Confession also calls on church members to pray that "the Lord would reward and repay [rulers] here and afterwards for eternity for all the privileges, liberties, and favors which we enjoy under their praiseworthy rule"—suggesting hope for their salvation.[14]

The Dordrecht Confession offers a revealing clue to the Amish response to evil by drawing a key distinction between the kingdom of God, composed of the church and those devoted to obeying God's will, and the kingdom of the world, which entails all the things in disobedience to God. Many other Christians also use "two-kingdom" language, but few use the terms as such stark alternatives. Following the early Christian theologian Augustine, most Christians believe that they live in both kingdoms simultaneously. For these Christians, the challenge lies in figuring out when one is required to act as Jesus would and when circumstances call for a less stringent standard. For the Amish, in contrast, the two kingdoms are separate realms. Baptism marks the step from one kingdom into the other, a rejection of the world and its ways.

For those committed to the kingdom of God, "the scriptures . . . leave no exceptions to the doctrine of nonresistance," an Amish doctrinal guide states bluntly. "Is it right to let others run over you without offering resistance?" the same source asks. The answer comes without a hint of ambiguity: "That is what the Bible teaches."[15] Not surprisingly, Amish expectations for the world are quite different. The world consists of both sin run amok *and* the worldly powers that seek to constrain it. The police and the courts, for example, may be trying to protect the innocent, but because they often use violence in the process, they fall short of Jesus' command. The Amish sometimes benefit from these worldly methods of constraining evil, but they are reluctant to participate in politics and government because the coercive methods of politics and government violate the teachings of Jesus.

Working with Worldly Justice

This moral framework shapes how Amish people respond to evil. God has instructed the church to judge matters of church discipline, they say, but worldly justice is the task of the world. In some criminal cases, however, especially those where the safety of others is at stake, they will sometimes offer testimony. In 2001, for example, Amish parents agreed to appear as witnesses in a case involving a non-Amish man charged with sexually assaulting minors in southern Michigan and northern Indiana, including a fifteen-year-old Amish girl. In this particular case, the prosecutor felt that Amish participation was decisive in obtaining a sixty-six-year prison sentence for the accused.[16]

When the Amish see an issue as a matter of conscience, rather than as a defense of personal rights and privileges, they may be more willing to cooperate with lawyers and use the courts. That was the case in the 1960s when Amish fathers agreed to be named as plaintiffs in a suit that led to the landmark 1972 U.S. Supreme Court case allowing Amish young people to forgo high school education. At various times during the twentieth century, Amish men have appeared in court, usually appealing decisions but occasionally initiating challenges to government regulations that run counter to their convictions.[17]

For the most part, however, the Amish maintain a cordial relationship with representatives of the kingdom of this world. After the shooting at Nickel Mines, for example, the Amish community expressed profound gratitude for the assistance of the Pennsylvania State Police. Following the dictates of the New Testament, they believe they should pray for governmental leaders, obey civic laws when possible, and pay taxes when asked. "What should be our reaction when we hear people complaining against the government?" asks one writer. "We should either remain silent, or where appropriate, reprove such complaining. We have much to be thankful for to live in a land of religious freedom."[18]

Even as the Amish express gratitude for the blessings of religious freedom, it is clear that this world and its ways are not their ultimate frame of reference. Humans respond to evil with self-defense or revenge, one Amish elder explains, when they "look back . . . toward earthly things and are not able to let them go in patience and Christ-like *Gelassenheit*."[19] According to this man's view, Christians should instead live with patient hope in a world to come. They should trust in God, whose judgments will eventually prevail in a heavenly home without evil and violence.

Of course the troubles of this world include more than just suffering from injustice and crime. They also involve other forms of pain and disappointment. The beliefs, practices, and affections of the Amish way help them navigate those human sorrows as well.

CHAPTER TWELVE

Sorrow

Sorrow upon sorrow, anguish upon anguish: that's death.

—AMISH FATHER *who lost a son*

I t was a splendid February day on the snowy slopes of western
Wyoming. Mervin Beiler and four of his Amish friends had arrived
from Pennsylvania the day before to explore the majestic terrain by
snowmobile.* Starting out on Monday morning, Mervin took the lead
for about thirty miles and then let others lead the way. He eventually
followed two of his friends over what appeared to be a small knob. But
the knoll hid a ten-foot drop on the other side. The first driver was able
to make the jump safely, but the second snowmobile hit fresh powder
and flipped over. Mervin, following the tracks of the other sleds, flew
over the knob and collided with the disabled sled, breaking his neck.

---

*Most youth end their *Rumspringa* activities with baptism, but a few continue them
until marriage. Some baptized young men water-ski, snowmobile, travel, and participate in sports activities even though these are discouraged by the church. Depending
on the circumstances, participants in such activities may need to confess them to
church leaders or the *Gmay* before they are married.

His friends came running, tried to check his pulse—and instinctively began praying the Lord's Prayer. Midway through their prayer, Mervin gasped and died.

About five hours later, back in Pennsylvania, Mervin's parents and younger siblings had just finished their evening meal. Some of them were washing the dishes, and others were singing around the table. Mervin's dad, Aaron, was sitting in his easy chair when a relative, who had taken an emergency phone call from Wyoming, came to the Beilers' door with the tragic news. "We all just cried and cried," Aaron recalled later in his memoir, *Light in the Shadow of Death*.[1]

Aaron notified his brother, and soon the house began to fill with church people, friends, and family. With the arrival of others, "the burden was made a little more easy," but even months later "the tears just flow as I write this." Mervin was Aaron and Mary Ann's oldest son, and his sudden death at age twenty-three was a shattering experience for his father, who spent several years struggling with his grief.

Sorrow is no stranger in Amish life. It arrives in the wake of accidents, fire, drought, and hailstorms that ruin corn and flatten fields of alfalfa. Sorrow settles in when infertility, miscarriages, and stillbirths occur in Amish families. It trails the death of a spouse, the failure of a family business, the decision of children to leave the Amish faith, and the shattering of trust. Sorrow, in its many forms, visits all human communities, but the religious outlook of Amish people offers distinct resources for coping with the heartache that accompanies tragedy and disappointment.

Life's Special Sunbeams

"Our blue rose, now gone, we hope is now blooming in Gloryland." That is how Emma Weaver describes her mentally disabled daughter, a special and rare rose, who died at twenty years of age. As a baby, Anna

166

"was a gift straight from Heaven. How we loved her. Her daddy was as happy as I was," even though Anna couldn't nurse, her eyes didn't focus, and she soon showed signs of other abnormalities. She eventually learned to sit, crawl, and walk, but her development was slow. As she grew older, she was able to help with family chores and enjoyed playing with kittens in the barn, teaching them to drink out of a pan. Anna attended an Amish school for special children, where she learned to read and write short sentences. She loved to give birthday cards to family members and friends, each containing a few short, carefully written sentences.

As Anna approached her twentieth birthday, her health began to fail. One morning she told her mother that there was an angel waiting outside her bedroom window. Emma wept, knowing that Anna "had her hopes and wishes in that great beyond . . . that eternal city where only Peace, Love, and Joy abide," yet Emma so desperately "hoped to keep her a long, long time." After Anna died, Emma consoled herself that "God had other plans."[2]

Genetic illnesses and disabilities can bring profound sorrow to Amish parents, but their faith helps them face these situations with patience. In the first place, they believe that the painful surprises of life always come with a purpose, even a message from God.

Parents of children with Down syndrome, autism, deafness, dwarfism, muscular dystrophy, and other disabilities publish *Life's Special Sunbeams*, a newsletter that is distributed nationally. In it, parents share essays in which they describe their challenges, exchange ideas and insights, and often reveal their heartaches. Threading through all the stories is a belief that having such a child, despite the difficulties it entails, is firmly embedded in God's larger purpose for the world. Speaking of her son with Down syndrome, one mother says, "We don't believe that the reason he is like he is, is because of something we did or didn't do. Ben is exactly in accordance with God's plan."[3] Indeed, the Amish commonly refer to children with disabilities as "God's special children."

As such, disabled children are considered special in the best sense of the term. One Amish-written poem, "Heaven's Special Child," describes a conversation among angels about where to place a child who will be born with disabilities. Significantly, these angels describe the child as "meek and mild," a phrase often reserved, in the Christian tradition, for the baby Jesus.

> Please Lord, find the parents
> Who will do a special job for you.
> Their precious child so meek and mild
> Is Heaven's very special child.[4]

Because children and adults with congenital disorders and other disabilities live at home and find work within the community, they are an ever-present reminder to those with whom they live to slow down or modify routines and expectations, and to include those with different abilities in the tasks of everyday life. Amish people are frank, often blunt, when they talk about disabilities, with little of the professional vocabulary found in polite quarters of modern society. But the belief that God places special children with specific families for a purpose fosters remarkable inclusion. Amish-published directories of those with disabilities typically list an occupation—from store clerk to "help around the house"—alongside each person's name, no matter how severe the person's limitations. This underscores the conviction that everyone has something to contribute.

A Legacy of Suffering

Amish people also look for divine lessons in personal suffering, whether it's the emotional suffering of grief or the physical suffering of painful or lingering illnesses. They believe that there is some purpose, however difficult to discern from a human perspective. And they believe that patience is important in the midst of suffering. "Whenever someone experiences illness, trials, or death," said a young mother, "we say, 'I wish you patience.'"

The Amish do not necessarily see human suffering as a virtue in the way that some other religious traditions might.[5] Nor do they invite affliction. "We don't go out and seek suffering just for the sake of suffering," our Amish friend Jesse explained. "What's the English word for that? Masochism, I think. At any rate, suffering just comes on its own in this life." And the Amish find plenty of examples of suffering in stories from the Bible, especially the life of Jesus, in the martyr stories of their own history, and in the hymns written by Anabaptists suffering in prison.

Heroes of the faith suffered, and Amish people often interpret their own suffering in terms of their faith. "As followers of Christ, we often experience suffering, because doing the right thing is not always easy," Jesse said. "Doing good often requires suffering, sacrifice, and self-denial." The twice-yearly communion services highlight the suffering of Christ. In fact, one member noted, "Communion emphasizes the crucifixion and Good Friday much more than the resurrection." Because Jesus suffered, members believe that they also should be willing to suffer.

But not all suffering is the result of doing good or demonstrating faithfulness. Sometimes it comes simply because we are human. "Misfortune, sickness, or suffering is also our cross to bear," explained Jesse. "To bear that suffering patiently without complaining is a good thing, a mark of faith." Aaron Beiler, grieving his son's snowmobile death, confides in his memoir, "I do not always understand why things happen as they do . . . [but] my little valleys are nothing when I picture Christ on the cross. . . . Forgive me Lord for complaining."[6]

169

A One-Arm Embrace of Medicine

Minimizing physical suffering, pain, and illness has been at the heart of modern medicine and health care. Amish people frequently use medical services, but often in ways that reflect their distinctive beliefs and habits. Because of the church's ban on higher education, there are no Amish doctors or nurses, so conventional medical care always comes from outsiders. Decisions about treatment are most often made by the members of a household, and it's not uncommon for families to mix modern and alternative therapies. They may, for example, seek mental health care from a self-trained Amish counselor, travel to Mexico for unconventional cancer treatments, and go to a state-of-the-art hospital in Cleveland for a knee replacement.

The Amish believe they inhabit a world empowered by the spirit of God, who intervenes to bring about certain outcomes, and they also believe that Satan seeks to distort God's plans. This does not mean that most Amish people think that illness is a result of personal sin or is some sort of divine punishment. But it does mean, as we noted in Chapter Ten, that they view nature as God's handiwork and that the more one embraces nature, the closer one comes to God.

Because the body is a natural organism, many Amish consider natural remedies to be uniquely in tune with the mysteries of God. So although Amish people generally accept the value of modern medicine, they do not grant it the sort of ultimate authority that many scientifically minded non-Amish people do. In Amish eyes, modern medicine represents human efforts to control the body, even prolong life, and they weigh those goals against their trust in divine providence.

Members of the most tradition-minded Amish groups make the least use of medical professionals, preferring either to treat illness with homeopathic cures or simply to accept painful conditions that others would seek to cure. They may wear a copper ring to ward off arthritis,

170

have their teeth pulled to avoid the need for dental care, or go to reflex-ologists to relieve ailments. A column titled *Ivverich und Ender* (Odds and Ends) in the Amish newspaper *Die Botschaft* offers a variety of salves and remedies that have been passed down in rural families for genera-tions. Coltsfoot tea, for example, is suggested for chest congestion, and hot lemonade is said to be a reliable remedy for colds.

The line between accepting suffering and inviting suffering, as Jesse put it, is at the heart of Amish debates over immunization. Most Amish parents support immunization because, as one man noted, "our feeling is that there would probably be many more sicknesses, paraly-ses, and deaths if no one took them." Said another, "We can think that our children will not get these diseases unless God wills, but are we doing our part if we purposefully neglect a preventive measure?"

In contrast, families in the most conservative Amish *Gmays* often ignore or resist public health calls to immunize their children. In a letter to an Amish periodical, a father in Wisconsin explains, "I feel we should put our trust in God rather than the technology of the world. I think God put these diseases here for a purpose, to chasten us sometimes." A writer from Ohio agrees: "We feel we need to trust in our heavenly father. Our forefathers didn't have the baby shots, so why should we?"[7]

Relatively few Amish households forgo immunizations, but even those Amish who make use of conventional medical practices usually refuse procedures that they see as artificially initiating or prolonging life. Amish families seldom keep a loved one on a life-support system for more than several days. In vitro fertilization is virtually unheard of, and heroic interventions for the elderly are rare.

Even the process of leaving the hospital can be uniquely Amish. A staff person at a large hospital with many Amish patients described with awe how "the Amish do their own social work." When a patient is discharged "we have an exit interview to discuss how the patient will transition to home care and therapy, and we may have as many as thirty

171

family members showing up. They are already doing different jobs to help the patient readjust at home. It's remarkable."

Anointing with Oil

Whatever the remedy, traditional or scientific, some illness and disease cannot be cured. In such cases, some Amish turn to a ritual of spiritual healing that involves prayer and anointing the sick with oil. Drawing on a Bible passage in James (5:14) that says, "Is any sick among you? Let him call for the elders of the church; and let them pray over him, anointing him with oil in the name of the Lord," a gravely ill Amish person, or that person's family, might ask for such prayer and anointing. The ritual is somewhat like last rites or extreme unction in the Roman Catholic and Eastern Orthodox traditions, although the Amish do not connect the oil itself to the forgiveness of sins as some other Christian traditions do.

The bishop and ministers typically read the passage from James, as well as Psalm 23, which is traditionally regarded as a psalm of comfort. They offer prayers from *Christenpflicht* and, if the sick person is conscious, pose three questions: (1) Do you desire this anointing? (2) Is there anything in your life you would like to confess? (3) Are you willing to surrender to God's will and whatever he has for you? After this, each of the ministers says a few words of comfort and hope. Then the bishop applies a small amount of oil to the patient's forehead and offers a final prayer.

The ritual is often as much a call for spiritual healing and comfort—a way for a dying person to affirm her or his faith in the face of death—as it is a prayer for physical healing. The Amish do not expect everyone anointed with oil to recover his or her bodily health. In some communities, Amish families readily work with hospice to allow family members to spend their final days at home. Hospice staff members report that Amish patients and their families are typically much more accepting of death than are members of the wider society. "They intuitively understand hospice philosophy: that life eventually leads to death," one nurse said. "They don't deny death or refuse to talk about it. And they involve the whole family."

Funerals Without Flowers

Although some Amish people die in hospitals or far from loved ones, as was the case of Mervin Beiler, most die at home surrounded by family members. This is almost always true for the elderly, who typically spend their senior years living in the *Dawdyhaus* adjacent to their adult children because the Amish do not use retirement centers or nursing homes. If an elderly parent needs long-term assistance with the activities of daily living, their children or adult grandchildren take turns providing the care. In some cases an aging parent needing continuous care will move from home to home, spending several weeks in each one.

When death comes, the funeral rites in Amish society express the final statement of surrender to God's will. Plain and simple in their ritual enactments, without flowers or elaborate caskets, funerals are held in a barn, home, shop, or tent at the home of the deceased, never at a funeral home or in a church building.[8]

Licensed funeral directors play a minimal role. In most communities a mortician transports the body to the mortuary for embalming, returning it to the home a few hours later. Very few if any cosmetic enhancements are done, even in the case of accidents. Speaking of the body, an elderly bishop said, "How it is, is how we take it." After the mortician returns the body to the home, family members dress the body and place it in a simple wooden coffin made by an Amish carpenter.

173

The community springs into action at word of a death. Relatives and friends assume shop, barn, and household chores, freeing the grieving family from daily tasks. Several couples from the family's *Gmay* or one nearby take the lead in organizing the funeral service. Women prepare food for the three hundred to six hundred people who are expected to attend. Friends dig the grave by hand in a nearby Amish cemetery and arrange the benches for the funeral service as they would for any Sunday-morning service. Friends and relatives visit the family and view the body at the home for two days before the funeral. They come by the dozens—often hundreds—to visit. "It's almost a social affair," said one person. There is a lot of silent crying and hushed conversation.

The funeral service itself is typically held on the morning of the third day after the death, although rarely on a Sunday so that the hundreds of people attending the funeral will not have to travel that day or miss their own church services. During the ninety-minute funeral service, ministers read hymns, Bible passages, and *Christenpflicht* prayers, and they deliver several meditations on death and hope. Singing is part of the service in some areas but not in others. Funerals are conducted in the Pennsylvania German dialect, but one of the preachers may offer his meditation in English if many non-Amish neighbors or coworkers are present.[9] A meal for guests may be served before or after the burial.

A horse-drawn hearse leads a long procession of buggies to a nearby burial ground, usually located on the edge of a field or pasture. A brief viewing and a short graveside service mark the burial. Pallbearers lower the coffin and shovel soil into the grave as a hymn is read or sung. Deceased carpenters and farmers, business owners and factory workers, housewives and teachers, dressed in prescribed clothing and lying in identical coffins, all have small gravestones of the same size, erasing social status. As a benediction, mourners offer the Lord's Prayer in silence. The prayer's petition, "Thy will be done," memorized in childhood and repeated thousands of times in life, seals the transit to eternity.

Death in Amish society has not been sanitized or segregated from daily life. Members of the family touch and dress the body. Children are exposed to the reality of death many times before they reach adulthood. Church members dig the grave and cover the coffin with dirt. Death is received in the spirit of *Gelassenheit*, the ultimate surrender to God, as the community reflects on the familiar words of a hymn they have sung since childhood:

> Consider, man! The end,
> Consider your death,
> Death often comes quickly;
> He who today is vigorous and ruddy,
> May tomorrow or sooner,
> Have passed away.[10]

In Heaven's Waiting Room

In the months that followed their son's fatal snowmobile accident, Aaron and Mary Ann wrestled with their grief and sense of loss. When Aaron saw some of Mervin's friends at a restaurant, he confessed to getting a "numb and weak" feeling. "And then I wonder why [Mervin died]?"[11] For people like Aaron who have lost loved ones, especially children or youth, praying "Thy will be done" does not suppress sorrow or banish the grief that accompanies death. To ease the pain, Amish people practice a number of grief rituals that publicly acknowledge death and provide emotional support for survivors.

Some who have unexpectedly lost a loved one gather each summer at what the Amish call the "Sudden Death Reunion." The gathering rotates among Amish communities across the country, and hundreds of people attend. The program mixes hymn singing with formal and informal sharing, as people tell their stories and console one another. "I have been comforted by seeing people comfort each other," one man said when attending the gathering for the first time.[12]

In most communities, women wear black when they appear in public after a relative's death. The length of time depends on their relationship to the person who died. This mourning dress allows others, even those they don't know well and who might not have heard of their loss, to respond caringly and offer words or gestures of comfort.

Visiting and sending personal notes after a death are strong traditions. Families that experience death can expect dozens of visitors in the weeks that follow and visitors every Sunday afternoon for at least a year. Sometimes guests simply sit in silence with the grieving, but often they listen, allowing family members to tell and retell stories of the departed and the account of the accident or final illness. Thirty-two families visited Aaron and Mary Ann Beiler on the first Sunday after Mervin's death, and at least twenty-five people visited each day for the following two weeks. With relatives, neighbors, or the visitors themselves providing the grieving family with meals, receiving so many guests is not seen as a burden but a blessing.

In the months after Mervin's death, the Beilers also received more than a thousand cards, with notes of encouragement from Amish friends across the country and from people they had never met. "Mail time was such a high time for me," Aaron said. On the first anniversary of Mervin's death, Aaron and Mary Ann received thirty-eight cards and numerous bouquets of flowers. "My, oh my, we are so blessed, Lord, to live in a loving community like this. . . . Friends and neighbors are bringing supper tonight for us."[13]

And yet the Beilers continued to feel the ache of loss and honestly struggled with their grief. Aaron processed his feelings through writing, another grief ritual common in Amish circles. "Hello, hello Mervin," he wrote, five months after his son's death, "I just have to talk with you. This is Sunday evening and church was here today. I have such mixed feelings. . . . Oh your friends, Mervin, you just would not believe the support they showed today."

Later Aaron wrote, "We know that all things work together for good to them that love the Lord. So what's wrong here? Who am I angry at? . . . Maybe I'm angry because I'm tired of crying. I cry so many tears . . . Lord, please help me. Please, God understand me. No, I'm not mad at you, but what's wrong here? Please take my anger away dear Lord. . . . Please help me, Lord."

The Beilers' feelings were complicated by the fact that, as a baptized member, their son should not have been riding a snowmobile, an activity discouraged by the church. One of the ministers in Aaron and Mary Ann's *Gmay* shouldered some of the responsibility, confessing to them that he had not confronted Mervin when he had heard, indirectly, about the upcoming Wyoming trip. The minister told Aaron and Mary Ann that he forgave Mervin's transgression and believed that God would forgive Mervin, too.

Human forgiveness and trust in a loving God are themes that surface in Amish discussions of sorrow, whatever its source. "God sees to it that the pain we go through does not get wasted. It is for our own ultimate good," affirmed Ben Blank, as he grieved the death of Annie, his wife of fifty-three years.[14] In a letter to Aaron and Mary Ann, Ben shared that during Annie's last year of life she had spent a lot of time in the waiting rooms of doctors' offices. She used the time to strike up conversations with people sitting next to her, some of whom found it difficult to wait patiently.

"She would remark to me later [that] she felt her life here was like living in heaven's waiting room," Ben says. "She wanted to make the best of her time here until the door opens and her name is called to come in. She never showed a fear of death because she believed in a God of love."

Annie's way—the Amish way—had nurtured her faith through a lifetime of patient practice. This fact didn't erase Ben's sorrow at the loss of his wife. It did, however, couple that grief with profound hope and trust.

Part IV

Amish Faith and the Rest of Us

CHAPTER THIRTEEN

The Things That Matter

What I had been looking for was the calm and focus
I felt when I was with the Amish doing the dishes.

—SUE BENDER[1]

Q uilts are the reason that Sue Bender, a middle-aged artist and therapist with two graduate degrees, ended up doing dishes with the Amish. Having stumbled upon some Amish quilts in a Long Island clothing store, Bender was so taken by their colors and design that she resolved to meet the people who made them, hoping to find something to fill the "starved place" in her soul. In *Plain and Simple: A Woman's Journey to the Amish*, Bender recounts her life-changing experiences in Iowa and Ohio, where she lived first with the Yoders and then with the Beilers. Although never tempted to become Amish herself, Bender insists at the end of her journey that her time with the Amish had transformed her in profound ways. "Through them I am learning not to rush through life in order to get the goodies," she writes. "Their way of life delivers the goods, and that is quite different."[2]

181

Bender is not alone in thinking that the Amish have goods to offer others. Secure beliefs, serene lives, contentment, supportive communities—all these things and many more have been identified as the rare and precious currency of Amish life.[3] The Amish themselves do not trumpet these virtues, nor do they advise the world on how to get them. Because they are more interested in living faithfully than in fixing the world around them, they have left it to outsiders to decide whether the Amish way holds relevance for the rest of us.

To be honest, we're a bit uneasy about attempting to patch up modern life by sewing on a few Amish values. The chasm between the Amish way and most of our ways is vast. Is it really possible, as one book claims, to "capture the simple peace of the Amish in your own life"?[4]

At the same time, throughout history people have borrowed many things—texts, principles, and practices—from other cultures and faiths in a sincere attempt to improve their lives. Even the Amish borrowed "Rules of a Godly Life" from eighteenth-century Lutherans, and some of them read Rick Warren today. If the Amish can do it, why can't we?

Benefits of the Amish Way

When outsiders mention what they admire in Amish life, they often list benefits that are enmeshed with what we've called Amish spirituality. Are these benefits just imagined? Some of them are, or at least they're overglorified. We know unhappy Amish people and have heard stories of discontented folks who left Amish life for the English world. Still, there are real benefits of Amish life that pull others toward them.

One benefit in the eyes of some outsiders is a *secure faith*: Amish people know what they believe, live their lives with conviction, and spend little time fretting over big theological questions. Of course, not every Amish person demonstrates this sort of steadfastness, but most of them do. Even teenagers, who sometimes test worldly lifestyles during *Rumspringa*, rarely abandon basic Amish beliefs about God, the church, and the Christian life. And it's common for people who are born Amish but never join the church to claim some Amish values.

Many observers also see *serenity* in the Amish way, a peacefulness they often contrast to their own lives. In *Plain and Simple*, for example, Bender confesses the frenzy that she felt on a daily basis. To her, the Amish were the opposite: even their quilts exuded a sense of calm. Bender's book may be unique in its candor, but many others also sense a tranquility in Amish life. "When it comes to living with an abiding peace," writes one author, "they are far beyond most of us living a frazzled, fast-paced modern life."[5]

A recent study suggests that this view is more than nostalgia for rural life. When researchers asked Amish and non-Amish women if they felt "overloaded," 50 percent of the Amish women reported no stress in their lives, compared to 35 percent of non-Amish women living in the same region.* In fact, more than three times as many non-Amish women reported feeling moderate or severe stress as Amish women did. According to this study, lower stress among Amish women stemmed from factors ranging from finances to friendships to family relationships. For instance, nearly three times as many non-Amish women felt significant stress in their friendships, and over five times as many experienced stress related to food, shelter, and health care as Amish women.[6]

Along with being secure and serene, the Amish strike many outsiders as *content*. This judgment, fostered by picture-perfect images of one-room schools, sturdy Amish farmers, and happy Amish children, can be overdrawn. Some aspects of one-room schooling may be attractive,

---

*This study surveyed a scientifically selected sample of 288 Amish and 2,002 non-Amish women of child-bearing age living in eastern Pennsylvania.

but probably not the lack of indoor plumbing. Farming is hard work, frequently dangerous, and economically perilous. Rates of depression in some Amish communities run about even with those in the United States as a whole, and there are also cases of sexual abuse.[7]

But although it's possible to exaggerate Amish contentment, it does seem that many Amish people have satisfying lives. Their own writings often list contentment as a by-product of plain living, which the study of Amish women confirms. For instance, 95 percent of Amish women said they enjoyed life most of the time, compared to 80 percent of non-Amish women. Fewer Amish women felt sad, fewer experienced crying spells, and fewer felt disliked by others. They also reported sleeping more restfully.[8] And if parents' happiness depends somewhat on seeing their children make choices they can affirm, then Amish parents have a head start on that score, too, because most Amish children join the Amish church.

A *tight-knit community* is yet another feature of Amish life that appeals to many outsiders. It's not unusual for an Amish person to have seventy first cousins, with many of them living within a ten- to twenty-mile radius. But it's not just biological kin who make Amish communities feel like a big family. The *Gmay*, a church where everyone knows your name, offers each person a profound sense of belonging. When asked if they have someone with whom they can share their concerns, Amish women far outpace their non-Amish counterparts. And they express more confidence than non-Amish women that someone will help them if they become sick or incapacitated. They also identify twice as many close friends or family members (ten versus five) with whom they feel at ease.

These four things—security, serenity, contentment, and community—sit atop the list of the virtues many people see in Amish life. At times wistful observers exaggerate them, but we are convinced they are real. Despite Amish aversion to boasting, many of them mention these same qualities when they talk about their way of life. Being Amish is not about seeking a good life, they are quick to say. It's about honoring God and living lives of obedience. Still, they would add, for those who remain faithful to God, there are blessings on this side of eternity, too.

Costs of Amish Life

The blessings of Amish life come with some costs, however. These costs can sometimes be measured in dollars and cents, but more often the purchase price is "giving up" of self. In that sense, the costs of Amish life involve things that most people are reluctant to lose.

The most obvious cost involves giving up self-determination. In the Amish world, the priorities are God, church, family, self—in that order. Given the church's view on living a godly life, to be Amish means forsaking many opportunities for education, career, lifestyle, and creative expression. Of course, many religious traditions rein in their adherents in certain ways. Rarely, however, does a religious tradition provide such comprehensive ethical guidelines for living. From clothing one's body to decorating one's home, from transportation to electronic media, the *Ordnung* touches many facets of life that most Americans, including religious ones, decide entirely on their own.

In addition, the *Ordnung* is actually enforced. Unlike many twenty-first-century religious communities, Amish churches expect compliance with their teachings. Once a member vows at baptism to uphold the *Ordnung*, there is no turning back without serious consequences. Should a member decide to leave, he or she will face another significant cost: excommunication and shunning. This prospect likely keeps some people in the Amish church who might otherwise exit. For them, the cost of leaving appears greater than the price of staying.

A related cost involves limited options. Consider the options that are generally closed to Amish children and youth: attending high school, taking music lessons, going to science camp, participating in youth sports leagues, watching television, playing video games, going to the prom, getting a driver's license. These limits continue into adulthood and sometimes become magnified. Without college, adults are blocked from pursuing many professions. They cannot design their own wedding ceremony, buy a house in a city, shop around for the most appealing church, engage in social activism, or enter politics. Amish men cannot opt out of ministerial roles, and Amish women cannot fill them. Most women are excluded from outside-the-home careers once they marry and begin to bear children. True, most Amish people, socialized from birth into the Amish way, accept these limits as part of God's ordained order and do not find them oppressive. Some, however, find the restraints hard at times.

Lack of convenience is yet another price of Amish life. The Amish accept some labor-saving devices, but they also reject many conveniences typical of modern society. We sometimes ask our college students, "If there were an affordable device that would cut your work time in half, would you buy it?" To them, the question is a no-brainer, and they invariably say yes. For the Amish, however, reducing labor is not always the highest priority. If it were, they would be plowing with tractors, driving to town in minivans, tapping the electric grid, and eating prepackaged foods for breakfast, lunch, and supper. Being Amish means limiting conveniences that most Americans take for granted. More often than not, such limits require more time, more sweat, and more patience.

Still another cost is loss of personal privacy. We've described the Amish *Gmay* as a community where "everybody knows your name," but it could just as easily be tagged as a place where "everyone knows your business." One of our friends who converted to the Amish told us that giving up his car was easy compared to losing his privacy. Accustomed to a life where no one cared what he did, he found it hard to live where everyone did. Non-Amish people in small-town America know something of this feeling, which the renowned storyteller Garrison Keillor depicts in his yarns about Lake Wobegon. But even in Lake Wobegon the social ties are not nearly as tight as they are in an Amish church.

We could identify other costs of the Amish way: a lack of ethnic diversity, limits on intellectual exploration, a ban on various entertainments, the prohibition of Sunday money-making possibilities, and so on. Our point here, however, is not to list all the costs of Amish life but to note that the benefits of Amish life come with costs—necessary ones.

Blessings Worth the Price?

Is it possible to have our "Amish" cake and eat it too? That is, can we gain the benefits of Amish life without paying the bill? Is there a tie between the gains and losses of the Amish way?

Consider the benefit of contentment. That, writes one Amish minister, is the "feeling of fulfillment and happiness that comes from . . . letting [God] decide what our needs are."[9] Many non-Amish Christians would agree with this man's sentiment, for it echoes an important biblical theme: God meets the needs of those who trust in God's promises. Amish people believe that their primary spiritual task is to align their desires with God's will. Of course, part of doing that for them means bending their desires to the dictates of the *Ordnung*: no cars, no designer clothes, no iPods, no satellite television . . . the list goes on and on.

From the standpoint of personal choice, the church's advice on how to live a fulfilling life seems constraining, but it also brings a benefit: it frees Amish people from feeling overwhelmed by choices and the pressure to consume more clothing and high-tech goods. "The fact that *some* choice is good doesn't necessarily mean that *more* choice is better," psychologist Barry Schwartz explains in *The Paradox of Choice: Why More Is Less*. Although Schwartz isn't recruiting for the Amish, he and other researchers have found that although most Americans are sure that having more options is the key to happiness, an "overload of choice" in modern societies actually contributes to "anxiety, stress, and dissatisfaction."[10]

This connection between costs and benefits is one reason the Amish are skeptical of seekers, the outsiders who trickle into Amish communities and ask to join. The Amish wonder whether these visitors grasp the full gravity of becoming Amish—whether they have done a thorough cost-benefit analysis. Some Amish communities give seekers a communal cold shoulder, though others may encourage them to move nearby, attend church services for a year, and test-drive their way of life. This testing time, which impresses upon seekers the cost of becoming Amish, usually results in decisions not to join. In fact, only several hundred outsiders have become Amish in the last hundred years, and some of those converts later left. For them, the blessings of being Amish were not worth the price.

More common are the selective seekers: outsiders who wish to borrow some benefits from Amish faith without signing up. They see virtues in the Amish way and hope to graft some of them onto their own lives without paying the full price of baptism: obedience to the guidelines of the church. Given the numerous books on this topic, it's clear there are many people who are drawn to the Amish in this fashion. "We don't need to 'go Amish' to bring true peace into our lives," assures one outside observer. "Their principles can be our principles," and "their peace . . . can be our peace." To validate her claim, this author cites the reassuring words of an Amish convert. Not everyone is "cut out to be one of the plain people," writes "Uncle Amos," but they can nonetheless improve their lives by emulating the Amish way.[11]

Learning from the Amish

But what does it mean to emulate the Amish way? What does it mean to adopt Amish principles? Although the Amish may have lessons to teach the rest of us in other arenas of life—how to start a small business, for example—we focus here on what they have to teach us about spirituality. The six ideas we offer are not quick and easy solutions, and considering our warnings about mending modern life by sewing on a few Amish values, we offer them in a spirit of humility. We think that these principles are both relevant and applicable for those who desire greater spiritual grounding in their lives without becoming Amish.

The first principle is this: *spiritual vitality comes at a price*. It's hard to imagine a contemporary religious community that asks more of its members than the Amish. To be Amish in twenty-first-century America is to be peculiar, an object of stares, curiosity, and sometimes even derision. Being Amish also demands a hefty spiritual commitment. Three-hour church services are only the tip of the iceberg, but they symbolize the serious way Amish people tend their spiritual lives. The high price of being Amish strikes some outsiders as the worst kind of religious legalism. We're not willing to say that, but we will say this: whether one is Amish or not, the cost of spiritual vitality is high, and those who pay the price are often perceived as paying too much.

The Amish way also demonstrates *the importance of taking spiritual perils seriously*. As we said in the Preface, spirituality offers resources for facing life's perils. Some of those are physical, some emotional, but others are spiritual perils that detract from people's sacred duty or purpose. Of course, what the Amish count as perilous may not strike their non-Amish neighbors as particularly dangerous. Amish or not, however, the principle is the same: spiritual perils must be taken seriously, and addressing them requires time, effort, and intentionality.

This leads us to a third lesson from the Amish way: *the importance of practices*. By practices we mean regular, sustained activities that involve the body as well as the mind and heart. Spiritual practices are everywhere in Amish life, pointing people to key spiritual realities and shaping their beliefs and affections in lasting ways. One Amish mother, Sarah, writes about teaching her children to sing old hymns long before the children could comprehend the words, for she knew that "repetition of the words [would] plant something in their hearts that will remain there for life, . . . reminding [them] of what is right."[12] The same could be said for other recurring practices in Amish life: preparing for communion, fasting, dressing in distinctive clothing, reciting the Lord's Prayer, kneeling on the kitchen floor to hear prayers read from *Christenpflicht*, participating in footwashing, and so on.

It's tempting to see these practices as mindless rituals, performed without meaning or passion, but they are actually rigorous training in the Amish way. Amish people know that the world offers many enticing paths to pursue, and each path has its own set of practices that shapes its travelers. For example, the life of a devoted shopper includes making regular trips to the mall, poring over circulars in the Sunday newspaper, and browsing online retailers to find out what's popular this season—practices that cultivate particular desires. If the Amish have anything to teach us in this regard, it's this: consistently performing certain practices—and forgoing others—is the most effective way to shape one's spiritual life. "The world is set on drilling its music into [our children's] hearts if we don't," warned the Amish mother. For her, family hymn-singing is an important form of resistance to the world's charms.

Related to this emphasis on practice, the Amish way reveals *the importance of patience*. Many aspects of Amish life force them to be patient. Amish people can't hop into a car to get a quick bite to eat, they can't surf the Internet to get the latest weather report, and they can't turn up the thermostat to heat a chilly house. It's not that they don't

190

experience these deprivations as deprivations, but their way of life forces them to wait—often—and in ways that would probably make the rest of us frustrated, anxious, or unhappy.

Amish resistance to a hurry-up world both shapes and is shaped by their spiritual practices. Rather than offering a fifteen-minute homily in a forty-five-minute worship service to satisfy parishioners in a rush, Amish corporate worship continues at its slow pace year after year. Their twenty-minute hymns do not hasten toward an emotional climax but deliberate on important themes. Ministers do not promise quick fixes to life's problems, and in fact they discourage members from sampling religious fare that promotes "an instant gospel."[13] All this stands in sharp contrast to American consumer culture, in which credit cards have replaced layaway plans and tweets span the world in microseconds. This culture of swift satisfaction offers consumers many pleasures, but it also breeds an impatience that can undercut spiritual vitality. In contrast, the Amish way reminds people that many good things in life come slowly, through practices that nourish everyday life.

If patience means proceeding slowly into the future, the fifth principle of the Amish way is its counterpart: *the importance of the past*. In fact, valuing the practices and wisdom of their spiritual ancestors—singing from the *Ausbund*, reading from prayer books, wearing traditional garb, driving horse-drawn buggies, living rural lives, and so on—is the most obvious element of the Amish way. Despite what some critics have said, these traditions are not dry, empty rituals left over from bygone days. Rather, Amish faith is strong precisely because it's rooted in practices that have proven fruitful over time.

At the very least, the Amish spurn the assumptisson that "new" and "improved" are always synonymous. As one Amish man likes to put it, the Amish "do not deny that change should occur but [think] that it should be checked by an experienced past."[14] Although the new may be easier and more pleasing in some ways, it may also be more shallow, transient, and less potent in shaping people's religious lives. Racing after the new may ultimately lead to distraction rather than spiritual depth.

Finally, the Amish way demonstrates *the importance of people*. By this we mean something more than friendship and camaraderie. We mean sharing in a common purpose, a common set of values, and a common set of spiritual practices. In Amish life, religious commitments are inextricably linked to a people, and the consequences quickly become clear when individuals abandon the community's way for their own way. More than any religious group we know, the Amish hold one another accountable to the community's purpose and the practices that sustain it.

It's unlikely that many twenty-first-century Americans would want to imitate the Amish in all their ways. Still, there are many things we can learn from them. The power of community in shaping religious convictions and habits is surely the most significant lesson for the rest of us. Sociologists are quick to remind us that our practices and visions are best sustained when we journey with a band of fellow travelers who share similar views and values. In other words, our religious beliefs are more robust and our affections are less fickle when we immerse ourselves in communities that deeply share and vigorously support a common purpose. It is difficult—indeed impossible—to imagine the Amish way apart from such a community.

What can we learn from the Amish? That a vital and meaningful spiritual life—one that enables a person to face life's perils with courage and confidence—is best nurtured in a supportive community. Few of us will commit to a community as costly as that of the Amish, and one marked by trust and accountability requires months if not years of effort. Yet whatever way we choose, the Amish way reminds us that the spiritual life is a journey best shared in the company of others.

ACKNOWLEDGMENTS

Supportive community, a theme so prominent in Amish life, was an essential part of writing and producing this book. We are grateful for the kindness and generosity of numerous people who assisted us with this project. We owe a large debt to the many Amish people who generously shared their time to talk with us. They patiently answered many questions and explained their spiritual beliefs and practices. This book would have been impossible without their insights.

Many other persons assisted us as well. We especially thank Cynthia Nolt, whose superb copyediting skills improved our text at every turn. Valerie Weaver-Zercher's editorial eyes sharpened our argument and enhanced our prose. We also appreciate the assistance of Sarah Biedka, Ambre Biehl, Steve Scott, and Julia Ward, who provided a variety of research and support services. As always, we benefited from the support of our colleagues at Elizabethtown College, Goshen College, and Messiah College. The Young Center of Elizabethtown College and its director, Jeff Bach, graciously provided accommodations and assistance for all phases of our research and writing.

The text of *The Amish Way* is more accurate and flows in a more lively fashion because a number of people graciously gave their time to read and critique drafts of the manuscript. We appreciate the thoughtful responses and critiques we received from Eileen Kinch, Christie Onoda, Jen Rankin, Ben Riehl, Craig Winslow, and two Amish readers who wish to remain anonymous. They raised good questions, and though we could not address all of them, our text is stronger because of their insights.

With warm enthusiasm, Sheryl Fullerton, executive editor at Jossey-Bass, and her team of colleagues encouraged us in numerous ways, and transformed our manuscript into a polished book. We deeply appreciated their professional expertise throughout the publication process. As always, our agent, Giles Anderson, furnished us with superb guidance and support as we negotiated the publishing world.

Finally, we are deeply grateful to our spouses and families. They provide us with unwavering support and affection, helping keep us balanced amid editing and deadlines. We are blessed to have such loving and faithful people in our lives.

Anabaptists, Amish, and Mennonites

The Anabaptist movement emerged in sixteenth-century Europe at the time of the Protestant Reformation. Sometimes called the radical wing of the Reformation, the Anabaptists emphasized a literal interpretation of the teachings of Jesus, especially the Sermon on the Mount. They rejected infant baptism, arguing that baptism should signify a voluntary adult decision to follow Jesus—and on that basis they proceeded to baptized one another into the movement. Because these radicals had all been baptized in the state church years earlier as infants, their detractors called them *Anabaptists*, meaning rebaptizers.

The Anabaptist call for a voluntary church separate from government oversight infuriated Catholic and Protestant religious leaders as well as civil officials and brought severe persecution. During the movement's first century, as many as twenty-five hundred were executed, often burned at the stake or decapitated. Hundreds more were tortured or imprisoned. This persecution fortified the Anabaptist view that the true church would always be a minority and produced a countercultural ethic of separatism. Small, scattered groups with diverse interpretations of faith and practice characterized the early Anabaptist movement.

In 1536 a Dutch Catholic priest, Menno Simons, converted to Anabaptism and eventually became a prolific writer and influential leader. In time many of his followers became known as *Mennonites*. A century and a half later, in the 1690s, another Anabaptist convert named Jakob Ammann led a renewal movement in Switzerland and the Alsatian region of France. According to Ammann, Anabaptists in his area had

195

become enamored of their social standing; he therefore encouraged stricter Christian practices enforced by vigorous church discipline. Ammann's followers eventually became known as *Amish*. Sharing a common Anabaptist heritage, the Amish and Mennonites have been separate groups within the Anabaptist family since 1693.

Amish and Mennonites immigrated separately to North America but often settled in the same areas. The Amish arrived in several waves, first in the mid-1700s and again in the 1800s. They established settlements in Pennsylvania, Ohio, and Indiana and eventually spread to other states. In the latter half of the nineteenth century, the Amish struggled with how to respond to changes produced by the Industrial Revolution, evangelical revivalism, and the encroachments of a mass, consumer-oriented society. During this time many Amish joined various Mennonite groups. The Amish who held to the older customs became known as the *Old Order Amish*. The terms *Amish* and *Old Order Amish* are often used interchangeably.

In the twenty-first century there are numerous Mennonite groups as well as Amish groups in North America. Although some Old Order Mennonites (traditional communities that formed in the late nineteenth century) use horse-and-buggy transportation, many Mennonites drive cars, wear contemporary clothing, support higher education, and use modern technology. Almost all Amish groups reject these things, and for that reason they have become renowned in the United States and beyond for their distinctive way of life.

District, Settlement, and Affiliation

Amish society is organized into self-governing local churches. The Amish refer to a church as a *Gmay*, which is a dialect form of the German word *Gemeinde*, or community. Each *Gmay* is defined as a *district*, with geographical boundaries marked by such things as roads and streams. The district is the socioreligious home for twenty-five to forty households. Amish who live in a particular district become members of that *Gmay* when they are baptized, typically between sixteen and twenty-one years of age. The close physical proximity encourages face-to-face interaction in daily life. Each church district has its own leaders—always men—typically a bishop, two or three ministers, and a deacon.

A cluster of church districts in a particular region is known as a *settlement*. A settlement might be small and contain only one or two districts, or it might encompass more than a hundred districts and cover several counties. The largest settlements are centered in Holmes County, Ohio (more than 220 districts); Lancaster County, Pennsylvania (175); and LaGrange County, Indiana (136).

Church districts that have similar practices and whose leaders cooperate with one another are known as *affiliations*. Unlike districts and settlements, which are geographically defined, affiliations are based on shared lifestyle regulations and church practices. Members within an affiliation interact together, often intermarry, and permit their ministers to preach in one another's worship services. There are more than three dozen affiliations of Amish in North America, each with its own distinctive practices. No central organization or national church authority holds the subgroups together; there are no Amish synods, dioceses, or denominational offices or programs. Most *Gmay*s in an affiliation have similar practices, but even so, the ultimate authority for Amish life and practice lies in the local *Gmay*.

Growth and Diversity

There are some 425 Amish settlements spread across twenty-eight U.S. states and the Canadian province of Ontario. All totaled, these settlements include approximately eighteen hundred church districts. Nearly two-thirds of the Amish population lives in three states: Ohio, Pennsylvania, and Indiana. Wisconsin, Michigan, Missouri, and New York also have sizable Amish populations.

One might expect a traditional group that rejects higher education, car ownership, and the Internet to be on the wane. Surprisingly, the Amish population is doubling about every twenty years. Counting adults and children, they currently number more than 240,000. Large families and strong retention rates propel their growth. On average, families have about seven children, but it's not unusual to have ten or more. Typically, about 90 percent of their youth join the church. Although the Amish do not seek converts, outsiders may join if they comply with Amish guidelines.

The Amish may all look alike to outsiders, but practices vary widely among the more than forty affiliations. For example, most groups have battery-powered lights on their carriages, but the most conservative affiliations use only kerosene lanterns. The vast majority of Amish homes have indoor bathrooms, but members in the most traditional groups walk to the outhouse. In some regions of the country, power lawn mowers are permitted, but not in others. The women in one affiliation may use only treadle (foot-powered) sewing machines, but those in another group may power their sewing machines with batteries or pressurized air. Some communities are wealthy, and others are rather poor. Even within affiliations and local church districts, technological and economic diversity is present. Racial diversity, however, is not. With very few exceptions, Amish people are Caucasian.

Religious practices vary somewhat from one affiliation to another. There may be recognizable differences in the order of worship from one subgroup to another, and in the procedures surrounding church discipline. Many affiliations are open to reading books and devotional materials written by other Christians, but members of the most traditional affiliations confine their religious diet to the Bible and old Anabaptist sources. An affiliation known as the New Order Amish is more comfortable than most with verbalizing faith and attracting converts from outside Amish households.

Technology

Many outsiders mistakenly think the Amish reject technology. It is more accurate to say that they use technology selectively. Televisions, radios, and personal computers are rejected outright, but other types of technology are used selectively or modified to fit Amish purposes. Amish mechanics also build new machines to accommodate their cultural guidelines.

The Amish do not consider technology evil in itself, but they believe that technology, if left untamed, will undermine worthy traditions and accelerate assimilation into the surrounding society. "It's what it will do to the next generation," said one bishop. Mass media technology in particular, they fear, would introduce foreign values into their culture. A car is seen not as immoral but as a harmful tool that would pull the community apart. Horse-and-buggy transportation keeps the community anchored in its local geographical base. Cars would bring greater mobility that would erode local ties.

Most Amish groups forbid using electricity from public utility lines. Electricity from batteries is more local, controllable, and independent from the outside world. In some settlements, for example, Amish use batteries to power LED lights on buggies, calculators, fans, flashlights, cash registers, and copy machines. Solar energy is sometimes used to charge batteries, operate electric fences, and power household appliances. Use of the Internet is generally forbidden. Some groups permit the use of battery-powered word processors, and one brand uses Microsoft software but does not have Internet capabilities. Some Amish people who work in non-Amish companies use computers on a regular basis at work. This practice illustrates the Amish distinction between using and owning technology.

Members of the most traditional Amish affiliations make very little use of telephones, though they may ask non-Amish neighbors to make emergency calls on their behalf. At the other end of the spectrum, a small number of Amish churches permit telephones in their homes. Most Amish, however, have settled on some form of limited phone access. They may permit phones in shops or other places of business but forbid them in the home, or they may establish neighborhood phone booths that several families share. Cell phones, popular with Amish contractors and with some young people who have not yet joined the church, are strongly discouraged in most *Gmays*, but are acceptable in others.

Amish use of technology often perplexes outsiders. Why would God frown on a telephone? Is it not hypocritical to hire English taxi drivers but refuse to own cars? And what could be the difference between 12-volt electricity from batteries and 110-volt current from public utility lines? These distinctions may look silly to an outsider, but within the context of Amish history they are important cultural compromises that have helped slow the pace of social change and keep worldliness at bay.

All these adaptations reflect Amish attempts to balance tradition and change. Economic viability often factors into their decisions about technology, but convenience for convenience's sake is not a high priority. The Amish seek to master technology rather than become its slave. Like few other communities, they have shown the tenacity to tackle the powerful forces of technology in order to preserve their traditional way of life.

Changing Occupations

Until the 1960s, most Amish people, regardless of the state in which they resided, lived on family farms. Amish farms were small, diversified operations with a dozen cows, some chickens, and a few beef cattle. Although many continue this tradition, Amish farms have grown more specialized, with dairy cows and, in some cases, chickens or hogs. Specialized farms tend to be more mechanized, but still less so than neighboring non-Amish farms. Farmers with more than twenty cows typically use mechanical milkers and bulk cooling tanks. The more traditional farmers milk by hand and ship their milk in old-fashioned cans to cheese plants.

Although farming continues to hold a revered place in Amish life, the majority of Amish people in many settlements have abandoned their plows. In some of the larger communities, less than 10 percent of the families farm. This shift to nonfarm work is the biggest change in Amish society in the last century. Still, despite their growing involvement in business and commerce, the Amish remain a distinctly rural people, living along country roads and on the outskirts of small villages. Many families combine off-farm work with hobby farming.

In recent decades, hundreds of Amish-owned shops have sprung up in some communities. Most are small family businesses with fewer than ten employees and are usually, but not always, overseen by men. The bulk of these businesses produce wood products—household and outdoor furniture, gazebos, small barns, and lawn ornaments—though quilt shops, greenhouses, and bakeries have also been very successful. With low overhead and an ample supply of family labor, the small home-based shops tend to be very profitable. The annual sales of the larger businesses may exceed $5 million.

Construction work also provides employment for many Amish men in some states. In certain communities, dozens of construction crews travel considerable distances to build homes and commercial buildings for non-Amish people. In other settlements, the majority of Amish men work in non-Amish factories located in rural areas or small towns. In northern Indiana, for instance, many Amish work in factories that assemble recreational vehicles.

The growth of nonfarm employment has brought new wealth to many Amish communities. Some leaders worry that the new jobs bring too much "easy money" and will eventually erode a work ethic built on generations of farming. Others fear that fringe benefits, such as medical insurance, that accompany outside factory employment will undermine the commitment to mutual aid within the church. For this reason, many Amish communities prefer home-based shops to "lunch pail jobs" away from home. "What we're trying to do," said one shop owner, "is to keep the family together."

Public Relations

The Amish generally do not join public organizations or service clubs in their communities. Some of them, however, are members of local volunteer fire companies and emergency medical units. Although they do not develop intimate relationships with outsiders or marry them, they are usually good neighbors who enjoy many friendships with non-Amish people.

Contrary to some misperceptions, the Amish do pay taxes: state and federal income taxes, sales and real estate taxes, and public school taxes. They are legally exempt from paying Social Security taxes, however, because they consider Social Security a form of insurance and refuse its benefits. The Amish believe that the Bible instructs them to care for church members who have special needs, including the elderly. To rely on commercial or government insurance would mock their faith that God will care for them through the church.

The Amish are taught to respect and pray for governing authorities. However, when caught in a conflict between their conscience and civic law, they cite the scripture verse "obey God rather than men" (Acts 5:29). From their reading of the New Testament, particularly the Sermon on the Mount, they believe that Jesus' followers are to be non-violent, and they forbid entering the armed forces. They do not hold public office and generally avoid engaging in political activism. Some, however, do vote. The rate of voting is typically low unless a local issue is on the ballot.

In recent decades, numerous conflicts have pitted the Amish against the growing regulatory power of the state. The points of friction have included military service, education, Social Security, health care, property zoning, child labor, photo identification, and the use of slow-moving-vehicle signs. To cope with these various conflicts, the Amish have formed a national steering committee with representatives in various states to work with legislators when issues arise. In general, however, the Amish have fared rather well in a political system that respects and protects their freedom of religious expression.

Blemish and Virtue

The Amish are far from perfect. Amish hearts sometimes swell with greed, jealousy, and anger. Parents worry about their children, and some Amish youth rebel against their parents, their churches, and even the law. Although the Amish forbid divorce, some marriages do sour. Church leaders have been known to abuse their power, and sexual and physical abuse occurs in some Amish families as it does in other North American families. Disagreements sometimes debilitate a church district, forcing the local church to split into factions.

Despite their blemishes, the Amish have developed a remarkably stable society. With little government aid, they provide care and dignity for elderly and disabled members. Apart from occasional arrests for alcohol or drug abuse among their youth, Amish communities have avoided many of the blights of modern life. With only a few exceptions, they have no homeless or unemployed members and no one living on government subsidies. Moreover, very few adults are charged with committing crimes. Thus, all things considered, the Amish have created a humane society despite their lack of high school education, professional training, and a full embrace of technology.

The Amish have learned to live with limits. Indeed, they would argue that setting and respecting limits on almost everything is one of the foundations of wisdom. Limits, for the Amish, are a necessary requirement for human happiness. Without limits, the Amish believe, individuals become arrogant, conceited, and self-destructive. To be sure, restraints diminish individual freedom, personal choices, and various forms of self-expression. At the same time, some would say, they grant greater dignity and security to the individual than the endless choices afforded by modern life. To the Amish way of thinking, a respect for limits builds community, brings a sense of belonging, and shapes identity—three important keys to human satisfaction and happiness.

APPENDIX II: AMISH
LECTIONARY

Although Amish ministers preach extemporaneously, their sermons are based largely on a lectionary of biblical texts that repeats each year. Families typically read the texts at home in preparation for the church service the following week. The texts are then read aloud in the worship service, either by a deacon or a minister, depending on local tradition. The church year begins with Christ's birth. Because each *Gmay* meets for worship every other week, there are only twenty-six weeks in the lectionary cycle.

Preachers make frequent allusions to Old Testament stories and psalms, but sermons are mostly based on New Testament texts. Within the New Testament itself, there is an obvious preference for texts from the Gospels of Matthew, Luke, and John, all of which present the teaching and ministry of Jesus. Of these Gospels, Matthew receives the highest priority.

In addition to granting such prominence to Jesus' ministry, the lectionary suggests other theological emphases, such as using a narrative-historical text (Hebrews) to discuss faith, rather than using a more abstract discussion of faith, such as that found in Romans. The readings also reflect Amish theological understandings as they relate to significant church practices. For instance, biblical texts that focus on communion (the Lord's Supper, or Eucharist) follow those that deal with church counsel and discipline, which in turn follow scripture readings on the new birth.

This lectionary is the one used by Amish churches in Lancaster County, Pennsylvania, since at least the 1890s. Lectionaries used in the

Midwest vary only slightly from this one. Please note that readings in the spring are movable to align with the dates of Easter and Pentecost.

1. Christmas
   Matthew 1 and 2, or Luke 1 and 2
2. John the Baptist
   Matthew 3 and 4, or John 3
3. Sermon on the Mount
   Matthew 5 and 6
4. On Judgment
   Matthew 7 and 8
5. Christ's Miracles
   Matthew 9 and 10
6. Christ's Invitation
   Matthew 11 and 12
7. Vine and Branches
   John 14 and 15
8. Easter
   Matthew 26 and 27
9. New Birth
   John 3 and Romans 6
10. Council Meeting
    Matthew 18 and 1 Corinthians 5
11. Lord's Supper (Communion)
    Luke 22: 1–32; 1 Corinthians 10:1–24, 11:2, and 17–34;
    John 6:48–71, 13:1–17
12. Faith
    Hebrews 11 and 12
13. Pentecost
    Acts 1 and 2

14. Starting to Bring in the Hay
    Luke 12 and 13
15. Harvest Time
    John 4 and Revelation 14
16. The Lost Son
    Luke 14 and 15
17. The Rich Man
    Luke 16 and 17
18. The Judge
    Luke 18 and 19
19. The Seventy Disciples
    Luke 10 and Romans 12
20. Autumn Seeding
    Matthew 13 and Galatians 6
21. The Shepherd
    John 10 and 1 Corinthians 13
22. New Birth
    Same as in spring
23. Council Meeting
    Same as in spring
24. Lord's Supper (Communion)
    Same as in spring
25. Faith; also Government
    Hebrews 11 and 12; Romans 13; 1 Peter 2 or Titus
26. End of the World
    Matthew 24 and 25

APPENDIX III: RULES OF A GODLY LIFE

"Rules of a Godly Life" (*Regeln eines Gottseligen Lebens*) has long been a popular devotional source among the Amish. Its origin is obscure, but it seems to have originated in European Pietist circles. Pietism was a spiritual renewal movement during the 1600s and 1700s, principally among Lutheran and Reformed adherents.

The tone and content of "Rules" is similar to some other well-known Christian devotional works, including *The Imitation of Christ* (c. 1418) by Thomas à Kempis and William Law's *A Serious Call to a Devout and Holy Life* (1729).

The earliest known edition of "Rules of a Godly Life" appeared in 1736 in a devotional book titled *Geistliches Lust Gärtlein frommer Seelen*—literally, "Spiritual Pleasure Garden for Devout Souls"—published in Basel, Switzerland. From 1787 onward, "Rules" has been included in various editions of prayer books compiled by European and North American Amish. The English translation that follows was done by an Ontario Amish minister, Joseph Stoll, in 2000. It appears in *In Meiner Jugend: A Devotional Reader in German and English* (Aylmer, ON: Pathway Publishers, 2000), 65–103.

Rules of a Godly Life

Beloved friend, if you desire to lead a holy and God-pleasing life and to attain eternal salvation after this time, then you must measure your

209

whole life by the Word of God as the only standard of faith and conduct, and let all your thoughts, words, and deeds be in accord with the same, as commanded by God (Deuteronomy 5:32, 33).

That is what the king and prophet David did when he said, "I thought on my ways, and turned my feet unto thy testimonies" (Psalm 119:59), as if to say, "I examine and ponder on all my doings—all my thoughts, words, and deeds to see if they are according to thy commands—so that if I have done wrong in one or the other, I can return to the right."

Part One
Concerning Your Thoughts

First of all, that which concerns your *thoughts*:

Take the following rules deeply to heart:

1. In the morning, awake with God and consider that this might be your final day. When you go to bed at night, you do not know if you will ever rise again, except to appear before the Judgment. For this reason, it is all the more expedient for you to pray every day, falling upon your knees both mornings and evenings, confessing your sins to God and asking His forgiveness, and thanking Him for blessings received.

2. Refrain from wicked, idle, and unclean thoughts. "Keep your heart with all diligence" (Proverbs 4:23). For whatever you allow your thoughts to be, your speech, your conduct, and your entire way of life will be the same.

3. Think often on the four last things: on death, of which there is nothing more certain; on the Judgment Day, of which there is nothing more terrible; on hell, for there is nothing more unbearable; and on heaven, for there is nothing more joyful. He who often thinks on these things will shun innumerable sins and be diligent in true godliness.

4. On the Sabbath Day take special note of the wonderful works of God—the creation and governing of the earth, and the work of redemption. To these meditations add the sacred practice of prayer, thoughtful attention to sermons, godly conversation, and such like. In this manner you will rightly observe the Sabbath and keep it holy as commanded so often in God's Word. If you however do not have a conscience against profaning the Sabbath, you will hardly hesitate to violate all the other commandments of God as well.

5. In all things, before you begin something, be cautious and ponder what the outcome may be. In all that you do and undertake, think constantly whether you would want to be doing it if that very hour you were to be called by death to appear before God's judgment. For this reason never allow yourself to be found in any situation in which you could not trust or hope for your salvation. Live every day as if you might die and appear before the judgment seat of Christ.

6. If anyone wrongs you, bear it patiently. For if you take the wrong to heart or become angry, you hurt no one but yourself and are only doing what your enemy would like for you to do, giving him the satisfaction of seeing how annoyed you are. But if you can be patient, God will in His good time judge rightly and bring your innocence to light.

7. Especially beware of discontentment or a spirit that is never satisfied. It is the grace of God that allows you to also have some suffering and trouble. God bestows on you various blessings so that you do not despair in want, but then He also metes out a portion of trouble and pain lest you become proud and presumptuous in too great a joy. No matter what misfortune strikes you, remember that because of your sins you deserve far worse.

8. If other people praise you for some virtue, humble yourself. But do not praise yourself, for that is the way of fools who seek vain glory. In all your dealings be honest—that will be reward enough and others will praise you.

9. Don't be overly concerned what others do, and if it is none of your business, don't meddle in it.

10. In suffering be patient, and silence your heart under the mighty hand of God with these meditations: first, that it is God's hand that chastens you; second, that it is for your benefit; third, that He will ease the burden; fourth, He will give you strength to endure; and fifth, He will deliver you from affliction in due time.

11. Never consider any sin as unimportant or of no account. First of all, every sin however small and insignificant it may appear is nevertheless a transgression against the supreme majesty of God. Secondly, a small sin that is loved can condemn a man just as well as a gross sin. A small leak if not repaired can sink a ship in time.

Likewise, even the smallest sin if it is cherished and not repented of, can bring a man down to hell. Beware then not only of great sins but of small ones as well. Make a habit of overcoming the least of sins so that you can be master of the great ones, too. Especially shun willful sinning lest you provoke God to anger, for it is hard to obtain forgiveness for sins that are willfully committed.

12. "Rejoice not when your enemy falls" (Proverbs 24:17). What someone else experiences may well happen to you by tomorrow. And anyone who rejoices at the misfortunes of another will not remain unpunished (Proverbs 17:5).

13. Carry no envy or hatred against anyone. The Lord loved you while you were His enemy, and therefore He expects you to also love your enemy for His sake. It is but a small thing for us humans to forgive our debtors compared to what God the Almighty forgives and pardons us. Even though you may think your enemy is not worthy of your forgiveness, the Lord Christ is certainly worthy of your doing it for His sake.

14. Do not esteem godliness any less because it is held in contempt and scorned by the ungodly. On the other hand do not look

more favorably upon sin just because it is so common, and the majority of the people live in ungodliness. Numbers are no proof that a matter is right. The way to hell is always full of wandering souls (Matthew 7:13).

If God should ask you on the Last Day, "Why did you profane the Sabbath? Why did you become drunk with intoxicating beverages? Why did you lie? Why did you live with hate and jealousy toward others"—would you then answer, "Lord, I did so because nearly everyone else did so." That would be a wretched answer! God would then say to you, "Because you have sinned with the majority, you must also be cast into hell with the majority."

15. If you are faced with an important decision in which you do not know just what is best to do or to answer, take at least one night's time to think it over. You will not be sorry.

16. Never go to sleep without first reviewing how you have spent the day just past, what you have accomplished for good or evil, and you will readily perceive whether or not you are making good use of your time, which is irredeemable.

Part Two
Concerning Your Words

1. Think that for every idle word you speak you must give account thereof in the day of judgment (Matthew 12:36). "In the multitude of words, there wanteth not sin" (Proverbs 10:19). So try to avoid idle talk and let your speech be deliberate, of few words, and truthful. Consider beforehand if what you are about to say is worth saying. Practice saying much in few words. Never state anything as true and authentic if you do not know for certain that it is so, and rather remain silent than to say something which may be false or otherwise of no value.

For when it once becomes known that you have no conscience against lying, no one will believe you even when you are speaking the truth. If however you love the truth, your words will be believed above the oath of a liar.

2. If you desire to be cheerful among honest friends, take care that your joy be not contrary to Christian love, nor to purity and respectability. Refrain therefore from rude insults and mockery that respectable people would be ashamed to hear. First, because such lewd words are an open testimony of an impure heart. "For out of the abundance of the heart the mouth speaketh" (Matthew 12:34). Secondly, smutty jokes and foul speech smooth the road to shameful conduct.

Indeed, you may say, "One has to have something to relate when in company with his friends to pass the time and to delight each other."

That is a wretched excuse. First of all, such mirth is clearly forbidden in God's Word. "Neither filthiness, nor foolish talking, nor jesting, which are not fitting," says the holy Apostle Paul—we must avoid them. Secondly, such lewd speech provokes the wrath of God (Ephesians 5:4, 6). Through suchlike evil talk and vain mirth the Holy Spirit is grieved (Ephesians 4:29, 30).

The tongue is the glory of man and the crown of all the members of the body. Shall a person then use it for obscenity? When the tongue is corrupt it defileth the whole body, filling it with unrighteousness (James 3:6). For this reason, loathe every kind of filthiness and let your speech be always pleasant and upbuilding, so that those who hear it may be bettered thereby. Use your tongue to admonish the sluggard, to instruct the ignorant, and to comfort the sorrowing. God will increase His gracious gifts to you accordingly (Mark 4:25).

3. Take special care to refrain from the vulgar, lightminded, grievous and shameful misuse of the holy name of God. It is certain proof of a frivolous, impious, and ungodly character to habitually profane

the name of God with swearing. Yes, it is also evident that he who constantly swears seldom speaks the truth. For if he has no scruples against the misuse of God's name, why should one suppose that he has a conscience against lying?

"But let your communication be, Yea, yea; Nay, nay; for whatsoever is more than these cometh of evil" (Matthew 5:37). In order to better avoid profanity, avoid the companionship of those who curse, lest you also fall into the habit. Rebuke your friend therefore, if he willingly accepts it. If not, there is no gain in rebuking a scorner (Proverbs 9:8).

4. Be not too ready to believe everything you are told, and do not repeat everything you hear. Otherwise, you will quickly lose your friend and gain an enemy. If you thus hear a complaint against someone or other, be sure to investigate the circumstances and only then give your criticism or opinion.

5. Confide to no one your personal secrets unless you have beforehand thoroughly proved him. Here is a way to test him and learn to know him: confide to him some matter of small importance, and thus learn to know him without risking harm to yourself. For if he keeps the secret to himself, it is an indication that he is to be trusted with confidences. Nevertheless, don't tell your friend everything, for if you should chance to fall out with him (which can easily happen), he will use his knowledge to your harm.

6. Do not speak evil of your friends. Rather, speak well of them in all that is praiseworthy. If they are at fault, keep it to yourself, for slander and scornful gossip are poison and a ruination to any friendship.

If you hear your neighbor's faults being criticized, search first your own heart before you join in. Without doubt you will find that you have the same, if not greater, shortcomings. Thus you will be moved to either better yourself or not speak evil of your neighbor, or belittle him.

7. When you are in need of good advice, do not seek first someone prominent who is highly esteemed, but go instead to someone who has

had experience in the matter in which you seek advice. Otherwise if some esteemed person in authority gives you advice and you do not follow it because you do not think it is good advice, you may anger him and thereby make him your enemy.

8. If someone with good intentions has given you advice which failed, do not blame him. For even good advice often fails, and there is no one on earth who can tell what the future holds. No person is wise in everything, or has enough foresight. Nor should you scoff at the advice of lesser men if they have your welfare at heart.

9. Do not make fun of another's weaknesses, but think of your own shortcomings (Galatians 6). We all have our faults and there is no one of whom it is not said, "Oh, if only this were not!" Either we are, or have been, or can become what another is. For this reason, have patience and sympathy with your neighbor's weakness and frailty. And yet, do not be a hypocrite by condoning him in his sin, or neglecting brotherly reproof and admonition.

But if you do wish to rebuke him, be careful to bring your reproof at a suitable time. For to rebuke others at the wrong time will do more harm than good, especially if the rebuke is too sharp and not tempered with meekness. A reproof is like a salad, in which one should use more oil than vinegar.

10. Make a habit of not replying to the words of others or to pass judgment unless you have first listened and understood well what they are saying to you.

11. You cannot have disputes and strife with your fellow humans and still stand in peace with God. If you love God, you will also love your neighbor according to God's will, who has commanded it.

12. Patiently bear your cross and do not complain to anyone. For your enemies may rejoice and other people will only think less of you if you complain.

13. Consider him a friend who privately rebukes you of your faults. It is a pitiful situation indeed if a man has no one who dares correct him when he has need of it. For if he is not rebuked, he may conclude in his own mind that he has no faults and thus continue in his sins to his own destruction, whereas by a friendly reproof he might be turned away from sin.

Everyone most certainly needs correction at times. For as the eye sees all and seeks the improvement of all yet cannot see itself or better itself, so by our very natures we are partial to ourselves and cannot see our own shortcomings and defects as easily as we can see those of other people. For this reason it is very needful that our faults be pointed out to us—which others can see so much more clearly than we ourselves can see them.

Regardless whether reproof is given justly or unjustly, by a friend or by an enemy, it can do a wise and understanding person no harm. For if it is the truth, it will remind you to better yourself. If it is false, it will serve as a warning what you should heed in the future.

But if you cannot bear to be corrected, then never do anything wrong!

Part Three
Concerning Your Works

1. Do no evil, even if it is in your power to do so. Take heed not to do anything when you are alone that you would be ashamed of before men. Remember with Joseph that even if no man sees, God sees all, and that your own conscience will testify against you. Therefore avoid all sins, not just those which are public, but secret ones as well. For even as God is righteous, so will He, unless you forthwith repent, bring all your hidden sins to light and set them before your eyes (1 Corinthians 4:5; Psalms 50:21).

2. Especially, though, resist with all strength of soul your bosom sin, or that sin to which your nature is inclined more than to all other sins. For one person this may be to seek the honor of men, for another a greed for money, a third may tend to drunkenness, a fourth to impurity, a fifth to pride. Against these evil sins you must above all arm yourself and resist them, for once these are overcome you can also easily master others. As a fowler can hold a bird by one leg, in the same way wily Satan can possess your soul and keep it in his control by means of a single sin just as well as by many.

3. If you desire to avoid sin you will need to also shun every occasion and opportunity of sinning. Whoever does not avoid every incentive to sin cannot expect to overcome sin. Evil companions are an incentive to sin, for it is from them that one often hears offensive talk that can easily mislead and corrupt a person. Evil company corrupts good habits (1 Corinthians 15:33).

Evil companions are the devil's dragnet by which he draws many into hell. For this reason shun such companions and have nothing to do with ungodly, lewd persons. If evil rogues entice you, don't follow after them (Proverbs 1:10). Whoever spends much time with evil companions is easily corrupted by them—he learns their speech and before he realizes it he gradually becomes like them. Among the evil, one becomes evil—he must either sin, or suffer. For this reason a devout man avoids the companionship of the wicked.

If you do not wish to be enticed to fornication or immorality, you must diligently flee from the place and the companions by which opportunity would be given to you to fall into these sins. If you would escape the sin of drunkenness (which is the broad way to hell), then don't become familiar with a drunkard or count him among your circle of friends. For of what benefit to you is such a person as a friend who would ruin your life, yea, your salvation? For experience teaches that more people have lost their lives through their own friends by way of drunkenness than have been killed by their enemies. So beware of all allurement to sin—you do not know how easily you could be deceived by the devil and by sin.

4. If you are tempted by evil companions or prompted by your own flesh to do any kind of harm to a fellowman, just stop to think how you would feel if someone did the same to you. What you would not want another to do to you, then likewise don't do it to someone else. "All things whatsoever ye would that men should do to you, do ye even so to them" (Matthew 7:12). No one likes to have others do harm to him, and therefore he should not do harm to others.

What you detest, don't do to others. If you do not wish to be slandered, then do not slander others. On the other hand, if you wish to receive favors, then show the same to others. Do you wish to obtain mercy? Show mercy to your neighbor. Do you wish to be praised? Then praise others. If this rule is duly regarded, all transgressions of the first and second tablets of the Law will cease.

5. When you in your vocation propose to do something, do not allow any misgivings about the providence of God, even though you are aware there is a lack of means. However, do not begin anything in your work without having first besought the Lord God's blessing upon your labors. For without God's blessings, all the diligence, effort, labor, and care that we humans of the household invest will be in vain and useless (Psalms 127:1, 2). On the blessing of God all things depend.

Pray therefore to the Lord that He would bless your labors and only then seize hold of the task with a joyful spirit, committing the outcome to the wise providence of God who cares for us and permits no want to those who fear Him (Psalms 34:9).

6. Never propose to get ahead or to support yourself by any means that God has forbidden, for what kind of gain is that if you have won it at the expense of your soul? (Matthew 16:26).

It may be that through illicit means you do make a profit, but in so doing you defile and violate your conscience. And who can bear the burden of an injured nagging conscience? Therefore, in all your dealings and business, be diligent as was the Apostle Paul to always have a clear conscience before God and man (Acts 24:16).

7. Do not be proud and overbearing even though you have been blessed with this world's goods, or else adorned with fine gifts of personality. For God who has given them will again take them away from you, if you misuse these gifts of His in pride and disdain of your fellow man.

Even though you may possess a certain virtue that causes you to feel proud, by the same token you have so many bad habits and shortcomings which give you ample reason to appear small in your own eyes. He who knows himself will surely find enough of his own faults to make it difficult to justify thinking himself better than others.

8. Strive to be an upright servant of Jesus Christ, not only outwardly in public services to hear God's Word and the religious observances of the Gospel, but also in your whole life by renouncing all sin and in true obedience to live according to all the commandments of God. Do not be satisfied when others think of you as being devout— but truly be in reality what you appear to be. Woe to the man who is not pious yet wants to be considered as such.

9. Do not think it is enough if you yourself serve God, if you do not see to it that all those in your care do likewise. The duty of a father is not limited to his serving God alone, but that he also urge the members of his household, his children, servants and maids to do likewise. For God has commanded this to all fathers of families, "These words which I command thee this day shall be in thine heart. And thou shalt teach them diligently unto thy children, and shall talk of them when thou sittest in thine house, and when thou walkest by the way, and when thou liest down, and when thou risest up" (Deuteronomy 6:6, 7).

So did Joshua, the gallant God-fearing hero, who informed all the people of Israel that even if they had no desire to serve the Lord, he and his whole house would nevertheless do so (Joshua 24:15). Every father must give account for the souls in his household just the same as the government for its subjects or the preacher for his audience (Ezekiel 3:18). He should therefore be deeply concerned that his wife and children, servants and maids serve the Lord God faithfully, which is the only way that their souls may be saved.

10. Avoid idleness as a resting-pillow of the devil and a cause of all sorts of wickedness. Be diligent in your calling so that the devil never finds you idle. Great is the power the devil has over the slothful, to plunge them into all kinds of sins, for idleness gives rise to every vice. It was when David was idle on his housetop that he became an adulterer (2 Samuel 11:2–5).

11. Strive at all times to be respectable in your clothes and have nothing to do with the vexing pomp and display of raiment. It is a great vanity to spend as much on one suit as would clothe two or three persons. If you in your old age were to think back to how much time you spent merely to adorn yourself, you could not but grieve that you ever loved such vain display.

Read often in God's Word, and you will find many warnings against pride. You will see that no sin was punished more severely than pride. It changed angels into devils, and the powerful King Nebuchadnezzar into a wild beast. It was because of pride that Jezebel was eaten by dogs (2 Kings 9:30–37).

12. Never do anything in anger, but carefully think it over first lest you come to regret it, and gain thereby a bad name. Meanwhile your anger will have cooled, and when you have again come to yourself you will be able to discern what you have to do. Always make a difference between one who wrongs you through lack of foresight and against his will, and one who does so deliberately and with malice. To the former show grace, to the latter justice.

13. Do not become too intimate with any man, except he fear God from his heart. For it is certain that any and all friendships, however established, if they are built upon any other foundation than the fear of God, cannot long endure.

14. Love your friend in such a way that you are not too confidential with him. This life is so subject to change and circumstance that no matter how a man conducts himself, it is hard for him to retain the good will of all his friends until the end of his days.

15. If you happen to get into any kind of dispute with your friend, do not despise him for it nor betray his confidences (Proverbs 11:13). For you want to be able to become friends with him again.

16. No one is his own master, only a steward over that which he has and possesses. Therefore, you must distribute of your goods to the needy, and do it wisely, willingly, and from the heart (Romans 12:13; 2 Corinthians 9:7).

17. If you are in a position of authority, rule much more with kindness and meekness than with fear and terror; for this is better than the use of tyranny, which is always accompanied by sorrow and anxiety. The righteousness of God cannot long endure tyranny—oppressors do not rule for long.

Remember that a harsh administration is a great injustice. God requires meekness from those in authority just as much as justice. For this reason, rule over your subjects with love and mercy so that they will love you more than they fear you.

18. Finally, in your conduct be friendly toward everyone and a burden to none. Toward God, live a holy life; toward yourself, be moderate; toward your fellow men, be fair; in life, be modest; in your manner, courteous; in admonition, friendly; in forgiveness, willing; in your promises, true; in your speech, wise; and out of a pure heart gladly share of the bounties you receive.

NOTES

Preface

1. The ideas in the next three paragraphs draw heavily from James K. A. Smith, *Desiring the Kingdom: Worship, Worldview, and Cultural Formation* (Grand Rapids, MI: Baker Academic, 2009). Drawing on the work of Charles Taylor, Smith prefers the concept "social imaginary" instead of "religious beliefs." See Charles Taylor, *Modern Social Imaginaries* (Durham, NC: Duke University Press, 2004).

2. Joseph Stoll, "Our Instant Age," *Family Life*, April 1994, 4.

3. This quotation is from "Letter from Birmingham Jail," which appears in King's *Why We Can't Wait* (New York: New American Library, 1964), 86.

Chapter 1:   A Peculiar Way

1. David Wagler, "Why So Different?" *Family Life*, October 1992, 34.

2. For two discussions of how North Americans view the Amish, see David L. Weaver-Zercher, *The Amish in the American Imagination* (Baltimore: Johns Hopkins University Press, 2001) and Diane Zimmerman Umble and David L. Weaver-Zercher, eds., *The Amish and the Media* (Baltimore: Johns Hopkins University Press, 2008).

3. Quotations in this story are from Don Allen, "3-Year Terms for 2 Amish," *Des Moines Register*, November 17, 1953; and Don Allen, "War Objector Found Guilty," *Des Moines Register*, November 13, 1953 (emphasis added).

4. Keith Elliot Greenberg, "Amish Painter Tries to Blend the Best of Both Her Worlds," *USA Today*, January 29, 1991.

5. Nancy Fisher Outley, "From Amish to Professional and Back Again," in *Perils of Professionalism*, ed. Donald B. Kraybill and Phyllis Pellman Good (Scottdale, PA: Herald Press, 1982), 44, 45, 48.

6. This story is adapted from Gertrude Enders Huntington, "Health Care," in *The Amish and the State*, 2nd ed., ed. Donald B. Kraybill (Baltimore: Johns Hopkins University Press, 2003), 167.

7. For an account of the accident, see Brett Hambright, "Amish Teacher Hit, Killed by Truck," *Lancaster (PA) Intelligencer Journal*, February 23, 2007, A1.

8. John and Fannie King, "Homer City, PA," *Die Botschaft*, March 12, 2007, 30.

9. Letter to Earl Wenger, March 14, 2007.

10. Elmer Schwieder and Dorothy Schwieder, *A Peculiar People: Iowa's Old Order Amish* (Ames: Iowa State University Press, 1975).

11. Joseph Stoll, "Looking for Loopholes," *Family Life*, July 2001, 7, 10.

Chapter 2:   *Spiritual Headwaters*

1. *The Complete Writings of Menno Simons* (Scottdale, PA: Herald Press, 1956), 198 (emphasis added).

2. Mary M. Miller, comp., *Our Heritage, Hope, and Faith*, rev. ed. (Topeka, IN: Mary M. Miller, 2008).

3. For a summary of the larger Christian tradition, see Alister E. McGrath, *An Introduction to Christianity* (Malden, MA: Blackwell Publishers, 1997).

4. M. Miller, *Our Heritage, Hope, and Faith*, 2. This quotation is borrowed or adapted from non-Amish sources.

5. See John H. Yoder, ed. and trans., *The Schleitheim Confession* (Scottdale, PA: Herald Press, 1977), 12.

6. *1001 Questions and Answers on the Christian Life* (Aylmer, ON: Pathway Publishers, 1992), 121. This quotation is taken from James 4:4.

7. *The Complete Writings of Menno Simons*, 198 (emphasis added).

8. Thieleman J. van Braght, *The Bloody Theatre, or Martyrs Mirror of the Defenseless Christians, Who Baptized Only upon Confession of Faith and Who Suffered and Died for the Testimony of Jesus, Their Saviour, from the Time of Christ to the Year A.D. 1660*, rev. ed. (Scottdale, PA: Herald Press, 1998).

9. Pathway Publishers, Aylmer, ON, issues a 1,004-page German edition of the book, *Der blutige Schauplatz, oder, Märtyrer-Spiegel der Taufgesinnten, oder, wehrlose Christen, die um des Zeugnisses Jesu, ihres Seligmaches, willen gelitten haben und getötet worden sind, von Christi Zeit an bis auf das Jahr 1660*.

10. Letter to David L. Weaver-Zercher, December 2009. The Amish-published German edition of *Martyrs Mirror* does not include the illustrations, but many Amish families own the English-language edition, which is illustrated.

11. John D. Roth, introduction to *Letters of the Amish Division: A Sourcebook*, 2nd ed. (Goshen, IN: Mennonite Historical Society, 2002), 12. For a general history of the Amish, see Steven M. Nolt, *A History of the Amish*, rev. ed. (Intercourse, PA: Good Books, 2003).

12. The Dordrecht Confession is also used by Old Order Mennonite churches. It is available online at http://www.gameo.org/encyclopedia/contents/D674.html. For a printed version, see John H. Leith, ed., *Creeds of the Churches: A Reader in Christian Doctrine from the Bible to the Present*, 3rd ed. (Atlanta: John Knox Press, 1982), 292–308. All quotations from the Dordrecht Confession in the text are from Amish minister Joseph Stoll's translation in *In Meiner Jugend: A Devotional Reader in German and English* (Aylmer, ON: Pathway Publishers, 2000), 8–61.

13. Harold S. Bender, *The Anabaptist Vision* (Scottdale, PA: Herald Press, 1944), 22–31.

14. *Ausbund, Das ist: Etliche schone christlicher Lieder* (Lancaster, PA: Lancaster Press, 1984). (First edition in 1564.) A handful of Amish communities use one of two variations on the *Ausbund* rather than the *Ausbund* itself. These variants, which were compiled in the nineteenth century, consist largely of *Ausbund* hymns but include some non-*Ausbund* German hymns as well.

15. "Song 34," in *Songs of the Ausbund* (Millersburg, OH: Ohio Amish Library, 1998), 1:73–74. Apart from this volume, *Ausbund* hymns are rarely translated from the German, and they are virtually unknown to non-Amish Christians.

16. Various editions of *Die Ernsthafte Christenpflicht* [The Prayer Book for Earnest Christians] are used in different Amish communities. The Amish of Lancaster County, Pennsylvania, have published this one: *Die Ernsthafte Christenpflicht* (Lancaster County, PA: Amischen Gemeinden, 1996). For an English translation, see Leonard Gross, ed. and trans., *Prayer Book for Earnest Christians* (Scottdale, PA: Herald Press, 1997). All *Christenpflicht* quotations used in the text are from *A Devoted Christian's Prayer Book* (Aylmer, ON: Pathway Publishers, 1995), selected prayers that were translated into English by Amish minister Joseph Stoll.

17. *Neu vermehrtes geistliches Lust Gärtlein frommer Seelen* [New Expanded Spiritual Pleasure Garden for Devout Souls] (Lancaster County, PA: Amischen Gemeinden, 2008).

18.   All quotations from "Rules of a Godly Life" in the text are from Joseph Stoll's translation in *In Meiner Jugend*, 65, 75, 85.

19.   M. Miller, *Our Heritage, Hope, and Faith*, 470–472, 474. The poem was written in 1927 by Max Ehrmann, a poet and attorney in Terre Haute, Indiana.

20.   Max Lucado, *Six Hours One Friday: Living the Power of the Cross* (Nashville: Thomas Nelson, 2004); Lee Strobel, *The Case for Christ: A Journalist's Personal Investigation of the Evidence for Jesus* (Grand Rapids, MI: Zondervan, 1998).

21.   Rick Warren, *The Purpose Driven Life: What on Earth Am I Here For?* (Grand Rapids, MI: Zondervan, 2002).

Chapter 3:   Losing Self

1.   See Jeffrey M. Wallmann, *The Western: Parables of the American Dream* (Lubbock: Texas Tech University Press, 1999), especially chapter 5.

2.   Robert N. Bellah and others, *Habits of the Heart* (San Francisco: Harper Perennial, 1985), 221.

3.   This quotation and the others in this section are from Paul Kline, "Gelassenheit" (notes, Holmes County, OH, n.d.). These notes later appeared, with minor changes, as "Gelassenheit" in Mary Schlabach, comp., *Message Mem'ries* (Millersburg, OH: Emanuel and Mary Schlabach, 2007), 147–153.

4.   "God's Beauty," *Family Life*, January 1982, 9.

5.   Here the Amish are influenced by Luther's German translation, which uses the language of being born anew (John 3:3, 7: "Es sei denn, daß jemand von neuem geboren werde" and "Ihr müsset von neuem geboren werden"), which has a slightly different connotation than the "born again" language in the King James and New International versions of the Bible. The best translation of the Greek is likely "born from above."

6.   "The Pangs of the New Birth," *Family Life*, August/September, 1984, 12–13. David Beiler, a widely quoted nineteenth-century Amish bishop, puts it this way: "It requires a serious battle to overcome and crucify this evil nature and put ourselves in subjection to Christ." David Beiler, *True Christianity: A Christian Meditation on the Teachings of Holy Scripture*, trans. Adelheide Schutzler and Isaac J. Lowry (Parkesburg, PA: Benuel S.

Blank Family, 2009), 230. For a more detailed discussion of Amish understanding of salvation, see Paton Yoder, *Tradition and Transition: Amish Mennonites and Old Order Amish, 1800–1900* (Scottdale, PA: Herald Press, 1991), 72–79. Yoder quotes a Canadian observer who said that, for the Amish, "the new birth was a command rather than an experience."

7. Nathan Weaver, "Amazing Grace: Is Our View Too Narrow?" *Family Life*, February 2010, 8.

8. "A Bridge of Many Stones," *Family Life*, February 1985, 12 (emphasis added).

9. Neither the 1632 Dordrecht Confession of Faith, which the Amish use as a summary of doctrine, nor the unofficial but widely used compilation *1001 Questions and Answers on the Christian Life* has a section devoted to the Bible itself or a definition of the Bible's authority. Nevertheless, both sources rely entirely on Bible verses to make their points. In Amish circles, biblical authority is assumed and not explained.

10. *The Writings of David A. Troyer* (Aylmer, ON: Pathway Publishers, 1998), 33, 101, 111, 123, 144.

11. "A Bridge of Many Stones," 12.

12. "Learning from the Tourists," *Family Life*, July 1979, 14.

13. "The Pangs of the New Birth," 13.

14. *The Writings of David A. Troyer*, 122.

15. "Learning from the Tourists," 13.

Chapter 4:   Joining Church

1. The story was based on an April 27, 2009, news release by the Pew Research Center's Forum on Religion and Public Life. The information was also reported by columnist Betsy Hart in "Church 'Hopping' an Insidious Trend," *Lancaster (PA) New Era*, July 5, 2007.

2. M. Miller, *Our Heritage, Hope, and Faith*, 218.

3. P. Kline, "Gelassenheit."

4. "A Copy Concerning Baptism," *In Meiner Jugend*, 189 (emphasis added). This is a translation of the wording used in most of Ohio, Indiana, Illinois, and throughout much of the Midwest. In other Amish settlements, the

baptismal questions are essentially the same, but are worded a bit differently. In all settlements, the questions are asked in German.

5. M. Miller, *Our Heritage, Hope, and Faith*, 304. The Amish find these qualifications for ministry in 1 Timothy 3:1–13, where they are outlined by the apostle Paul.

6. [Joseph F. Beiler], "Ordnung," *Mennonite Quarterly Review* 56, no. 4 (October 1982): 384.

7. "The Ordnung as Agreed on When Top Buggies Came In," *Die Kurier*, February 10, 1998. This newsletter serves the Amish community in Daviess County, Indiana.

8. "Teach Your Children to Sing," *Family Life*, January 1995, 18.

9. All the Beiler quotations in this section are from [J. Beiler], "Ordnung," 382–384.

10. Joe Keim, response to a letter to the editor, *The Plain Truth: Christianity Without the Religion* 71, no. 4 (July/August 2006), 3, http://ptm.org/06PT/JulAug/contents.pdf.

11. [J. Beiler], "Ordnung," 384.

12. "A Bridge of Many Stones," 13.

13. [J. Beiler], "Ordnung," 382.

Chapter 5: Worshiping God

1. Although some observers describe Amish singing as a Gregorian chant, it is more like Torah chanting. For background on the *Ausbund* and the Amish style of singing, see Hedwig Durnbaugh, "The Amish Singing Style: Theories of Its Origin and Description of Its Singularity," *Pennsylvania Mennonite Heritage* 22, no. 2 (April 1999): 24–31, and David Luthy, "Four Centuries with the *Ausbund*," *Family Life*, June 1971, 21–22.

2. P. Kline, "Gelassenheit."

3. M. Miller, *Our Heritage, Hope, and Faith*, 115; original in the *Ausbund, Das ist*, 770 (hymn no. 131).

4. "Risting for Gmay," *The Diary*, March 2009, 1.

5. Samuel S. Stoltzfus, "Going in with the Boys," *Pennsylvania Mennonite Heritage* 31, no. 1 (January 2008): 31–32.

6. P. Kline, "Gelassenheit."

7. P. Kline, "Gelassenheit."

8. "A Bridge of Many Stones," 12.

9. P. Kline, "Gelassenheit."

10. M. Miller, *Our Heritage, Hope, and Faith*, 251 (altered for clarity).

11. M. Miller, *Our Heritage, Hope, and Faith*, 268.

12. This quotation and the next two are from *Handbuch für Bischof* [Handbook for Bishop] (Gordonville, PA: Gordonville Print Shop, 1978), 20–21. English translation by Noah G. Good.

13. "Dordrecht Confession, Article 11," *In Meiner Jugend*, 41.

Chapter 6: *Living Together*

1. Elmo Stoll, "Five Reasons for Church Splits," *Family Life*, February 1992, 11.

2. Some business owners do carry commercial fire insurance or product liability (or both) to cover damages suffered by customers. In 1965 the U.S. Congress exempted Amish people from participation in Social Security, including Medicare and Medicaid. In a few cases, some Amish employees in non-Amish businesses do participate in Social Security. For a history of these exemptions and other twentieth-century Amish conflicts with the state, see Donald B. Kraybill, ed., *The Amish and the State*, 2nd ed. (Baltimore: Johns Hopkins University Press, 2003).

3. *1001 Questions and Answers*, 154, 155.

4. In many Amish communities, networks of local congregations organize mutual aid plans with premiums. These plans have rather large deductibles and then pay about three-fourths of the remaining bills, with limits. See "The Tables of the Money Changers," *Family Life*, July 1992, 25.

5. Elmo Stoll, "Is Insurance Right or Wrong?" *Family Life*, April 1984, 11.

6. *The Budget* (Sugarcreek, OH), March 3, 2004, 19.

7. For more detail on church discipline rituals, see Donald B. Kraybill, *The Riddle of Amish Culture*, rev. ed. (Baltimore: Johns Hopkins University Press, 2001), 131–141.

8. "A Timely Letter [by Samuel J. Beachy, July 1992]," *The Diary*, April 1993, 37.

9.   M. Miller, *Our Heritage, Hope, and Faith*, 379.

10. M. Miller, *Our Heritage, Hope, and Faith*, 378–379.

11. D. Kraybill, *The Riddle of Amish Culture*, 135.

12. For a discussion of different patterns and practices of shunning, see Steven M. Nolt and Thomas J. Meyers, *Plain Diversity: Amish Cultures and Identities* (Baltimore: Johns Hopkins University Press, 2007), 46–47, 106, 111–112.

13. Elmo Stoll, "The Doctrine Most Churches Shun," *Family Life*, May 1980, 10.

14. Ruth Irene Garrett and Rick Farrant, *Crossing Over: One Woman's Escape from Amish Life* (New York: HarperCollins, 2003), 2.

15. Ottie Garrett, ed., *True Stories of the X-Amish* (Horse Cave, KY: Neu Leben, 1998); Mission to Amish People (http://www.mapministry.org/).

16. E. Stoll, "The Doctrine Most Churches Shun," 10.

17. R. Garrett and R. Farrant, *Crossing Over*, 2.

18. All quotations related to this story are from "A Timely Letter" [by Samuel J. Beachy, July 1992], 36–38. Another published account of someone returning to the church is in *Indiana Amish Directory: Elkhart, LaGrange, and Noble Counties, 2007* (Middlebury, IN: J. E. Miller, 2007), 9–10, concerning Christian J. Miller (1890–1970), who left the Amish church in 1917 and joined another denomination, where he was ordained. When he returned to the Amish church, it recognized his ordination.

Chapter 7:   Children

1.   Kirk Miller and others, "Health Status, Health Conditions, and Health Behaviors Among Amish Women: Results from the Central Pennsylvania Women's Health Study (CePAWHS)," *Women's Health Issues* 17 (2007): 168.

2.   A few church districts (less than 5 percent) hold Sunday school on their off-Sundays, but they are exceptions.

3.   *1001 Questions and Answers*, 101.

4.   "Rules of a Godly Life," *In Meiner Jugend*, 97.

5.   Widely quoted in Amish communities, "Die Kinder Zucht" (Anonymous) appeared as a full-page spread in *The Grapevine*, a newsletter serving the Iowa Amish communities, April 2, 2008, 6. English translation by Walton Z. Moyer.

6. "A Most Sacred Call," *Lancaster Gemeinde Brief*, November 5, 2009, 11. This newsletter serves the Amish community in Lancaster, Pennsylvania.

7. "Teach Your Children to Sing," 17.

8. *Das Neue Kinder Lieder: Ein Gesangbuch fur Schulen und Heimaten* (Aylmer, ON: Pathway Publishers, 1972), song no. 4. All translations from this book are by Walton Z. Moyer.

9. Sam S. Stoltzfus, "Our Plain Folks and Their Spirituality," *The Connection*, August 2009, 55.

10. "Teach Your Children to Sing," 17.

11. *School Favorites: Around 110 of Our Favorite Songs* (Gordonville, PA: Gordonville Print Shop, 1980), 9.

12. "The Cruelest Kind of Child Abuse," *Family Life*, January 1995, 6.

13. *1001 Questions and Answers*, 100.

14. This quotation and the one in the following paragraph are from "The Cruelest Kind of Child Abuse," 6–7.

15. "Tips on Training a Two-Year-Old," *Family Life*, August/September 2009, 12.

16. "Rules of a Godly Life," *In Meiner Jugend*, 99.

17. Chris Stoll, "Honey from the Rock," *Farming Magazine*, Spring 2003, 15, 14.

18. "Tips on Training a Two-Year-Old," 12.

19. Donald B. Kraybill and Steven M. Nolt, *Amish Enterprise*, 2nd ed. (Baltimore: Johns Hopkins University Press, 2004), 212.

20. *Standards of the Old Order Amish and Old Order Mennonite Parochial and Vocational Schools of Pennsylvania* (Old Order Book Society, 1988; repr., Gordonville, PA: Gordonville Print Shop, 2006), 2.

21. This quotation and the next are from S. Stoltzfus, "Our Plain Folks and Their Spirituality," 51, 55.

22. "Teach Your Children to Sing," 18.

23. S. Stoltzfus, "Going in with the Boys," 32.

Chapter 8: Family

1. This prayer and the prayer in the next paragraph are from *A Devoted Christian's Prayer Book* (Aylmer, ON: Pathway Publishers, 1995), 15–17,

13–15. This volume contains selected prayers from *Die Ernsthafte Christenpflicht* that were translated into English by Amish minister Joseph Stoll.

2. Mrs. Melvin [Esther] Lapp, comp., *Heartland Hymns* (Paradise, PA: Esther Lapp, 2005).

3. Hilde E. Binford, "Values and Culture Transmitted Through Music in the Old Order Amish Community" (unpublished paper, n.d.), 1.

4. The best overview of Amish weddings is found in Richard A. Stevick, *Growing Up Amish: The Teenage Years* (Baltimore: Johns Hopkins University Press, 2007), 199–228. Stephen Scott, in *The Amish Wedding and Other Special Occasions of the Old Order Communities* (Intercourse, PA: Good Books, 1988), 4–35, describes a traditional wedding in Lancaster County as well as different practices in other settlements. A careful description of three weddings appears in Pauline Stevick, *Beyond the Plain and Simple: A Patchwork of Amish Lives* (Kent, OH: Kent State University Press, 2006), 47–58.

5. M. Miller, *Our Heritage, Hope, and Faith*, 243–288, lists all the songs, prayers, and scripture readings that are appropriate for the church service preceding a wedding.

6. "A Copy Concerning Matrimony," *In Meiner Jugend*, 211. The wording of marriage vows varies somewhat among settlements. The vows here are those used in Ohio and Indiana.

7. *1001 Questions and Answers*, 96–97.

8. Charles E. Hurst and David L. McConnell, *An Amish Paradox: Diversity and Change in the World's Largest Amish Community* (Baltimore: Johns Hopkins University Press, 2010), 122.

9. *1001 Questions and Answers*, 97.

10. This quotation and the one in the next paragraph are from Hurst and McConnell, *An Amish Paradox*, 121, 125.

11. *The Doorway to Hope for the Hurting, Struggling and Discouraged* (Fort Wayne, IN: The Sewing Circle, n.d.).

12. K. Miller and others, "Health Status," 167.

13. Marc A. Olshan and Kimberly D. Schmidt, "Amish Women and the Feminist Conundrum," in *The Amish Struggle with Modernity*, ed. Donald B.

Kraybill and Marc A. Olshan (Hanover, NH: University Press of New England, 1994), 229.

14. Mrs. Jerre S. [Ruthie] Esh, comp., *A Collection of Treasured Recipes and Poems from the Esh Family* (Christiana, PA: Mrs. Jerre S. [Ruthie] Esh, n.d.), 20.

15. "Teach Your Children to Sing," 17.

16. S. Stoltzfus, "Our Plain Folks and Their Spirituality," 51.

17. David Bontrager, "Bridging the Generation Gap," *Farming Magazine*, Spring 2009, 16.

Chapter 9: *Possessions*

1. [Elmo Stoll], *Strangers and Pilgrims: Why We Live Simply* (Aylmer, ON: Pathway Publishers, 2008), 8.

2. [E. Stoll], *Strangers and Pilgrims*, 3–9.

3. *1001 Questions and Answers*, 141.

4. David Wagler, *Are All Things Lawful?* (Aylmer, ON: Pathway Publishers, n.d.), 7.

5. [E. Stoll], *Strangers and Pilgrims*, 5.

6. "Rules of a Godly Life," *In Meiner Jugend*, 89.

7. [Ben Blank], *The Amazing Story of the Ausbund* (Narvon, PA: Benuel S. Blank, 2001), 45.

8. All the quotations in this section and the next are from *1001 Questions and Answers*, 141–143.

9. This quotation and the one in the next paragraph are from "Staff Notes," *Family Life*, July 1994, 4–5.

10. The quotations in this and the next paragraph are from *1001 Questions and Answers*, 130–131.

11. P. Kline, "Gelassenheit."

12. Elmo Stoll, "Cheap Shirts and Shallow Reasoning," *Family Life*, January 1972, 12.

13. P. Kline, "Gelassenheit."

14. This quotation and the one in the next paragraph are from "Simple Living: How Can We Keep It?" *Family Life*, May 1997, 18–19.

15. *1001 Questions and Answers*, 155.

16. Ben Blank, *The Scriptures Have the Answers: Inspirational Writings by Ben Blank* (Parkesburg, PA: Blank Family, 2009), 155.

17. "Simple Living," 18.

Chapter 10: Nature

1. *1001 Questions and Answers*, 138–139.

2. "Dordrecht Confession, Article 1," *In Meiner Jugend*, 11.

3. [Ben Blank], *Creation to Resurrection: A History of Bible Times* (Narvon, PA: Benuel S. Blank, 2005), 11.

4. *1001 Questions and Answers*, 162.

5. [B. Blank], *Creation to Resurrection*, 11.

6. David Kline, "God's Spirit and a Theology for Living," in *Creation and the Environment: An Anabaptist Perspective on a Sustainable World*, ed. Calvin Redekop (Baltimore: Johns Hopkins University Press, 2000), 65.

7. *1001 Questions and Answers*, 139.

8. "Out in the Fields with God," *The Diary*, June 2008, 113.

9. David Kline, editorial in *Farming Magazine*, Summer 2009, 7.

10. David Kline and others, "Honouring Creation and Tending the Garden: Amish Views of Biodiversity," in *Cultural and Spiritual Values of Biodiversity*, ed. Darrell Addison Posey (London: Intermediate Technology Publications, 1999), 309.

11. Elsie Kline, "The Farm Home," *Farming Magazine*, Spring 2005, 43.

12. Katie Troyer, "The Garden Path," *Farming Magazine*, Spring 2002, 44.

13. Richard Louv, *Last Child in the Woods: Saving Our Children from Nature-Deficit Disorder*, rev. ed. (Chapel Hill, NC: Algonquin Books of Chapel Hill, 2008), 117, 31.

14. David Kline, editorial in *Farming Magazine*, Spring 2007, 7.

15. *Arithmetic Grade Six* (Shipshewana, IN: Study Time Publishers, 2001), 137.

16. *Plain Connection*, September 2009, 1. This newsletter serves the Amish communities of Minnesota and Wisconsin.

17. David Kline, *Scratching the Woodchuck: Nature on an Amish Farm* (Athens: University of Georgia Press, 1997), 179.

18. "The Danger of Horsepower," *Family Life*, December 1980, 18.

19.   David Kline, public lecture at Horse Progress Days exhibition, Lebanon, Pennsylvania, July 2005.

20.   D. Kline, "God's Spirit and a Theology for Living," 61–62.

21.   David Kline, editorial in *Farming Magazine*, Spring 2004, 7.

22.   "Learning from the Tourists," 14.

23.   D. Kline, editorial in *Farming Magazine*, Spring 2004, 7.

24.   *Grass-Based Dairy Farming* (Sugarcreek, OH: privately published, 2008), v.

25.   This quotation and the next are from D. Kline, "God's Spirit and a Theology for Living," 69, 66–67.

Chapter 11:   Evil

1.   "Few Amish Victims Report Crimes," *South Bend Tribune*, February 13, 1996, A-1, A-2; "Amish Forgiving in Wake of Attempted Assaults," *South Bend Tribune*, August 28, 1996, A-1, A-2; "Witnesses Crucial to Convicting 'Amo-bashers,'" *South Bend Tribune*, August 28, 1996, A-2.

2.   *1001 Questions and Answers*, 10–11.

3.   D. Beiler, *True Christianity*, 115.

4.   "Dordrecht Confession of Faith, Article 14," *In Meiner Jugend*, 47.

5.   Sarah Jean Yoder, *Benjie, the In-Between Boy* (Aylmer, ON: Pathway Publishers, 1995), 72, 75.

6.   Daniel L. Migliore, *Faith Seeking Understanding: An Introduction to Christian Theology*, 2nd ed. (Grand Rapids, MI: Eerdmans, 2004), 421.

7.   John A. N. Troyer, "John A. N. Troyer," in *Beyond the Valley: Over 110 Stories of People Who Are Physically Challenged* (Monroe, IN: Hilty Home Sales, 2005), 417–419.

8.   Ada E. Borkholder, "Ada E. Borkholder," in *Beyond the Valley*, 22–23.

9.   John A. Hostetler, *Amish Society*, 4th ed. (Baltimore: Johns Hopkins University Press, 1993), 389.

10.   *1001 Questions and Answers*, 160.

11.   S. Yoder, *Benjie*, 73.

12.   Cindy Stauffer and Janet Kelley, "A Boy's Death, a Family's Forgiveness," *Lancaster (PA) New Era*, September 25, 2006, A1.

13.   This quotation and two others in this section are from "The Need of Forgiving," *Family Life*, October 1985, 10.

14. "Dordrecht Confession of Faith, Article 13," *In Meiner Jugend*, 45, 47.

15. *1001 Questions and Answers*, 146.

16. "Plea Ends Molestation Trial," *Elkhart (IN) Truth*, March 15, 2001, A-1, A-10; "Child Molester Sentenced to a 66-Year Prison Term," *Goshen (IN) News*, May 2, 2001, A-1, A-2.

17. D. Kraybill, ed., *The Amish and the State*.

18. *1001 Questions and Answers*, 157.

19. D. Beiler, *True Christianity*, 132.

Chapter 12: Sorrow

1. [Aaron Beiler], *Light in the Shadow of Death* (New Holland, PA: Aaron Beiler, 2008).

2. *Life's Special Sunbeams*, February 2010, 5–7.

3. *Life's Special Sunbeams*, March 2010, 6.

4. Anonymous, *Life's Special Sunbeams*, March 2010, 2.

5. Robert A. Orsi, "'Mildred, Is It Fun to Be a Cripple?' The Culture of Suffering in Mid-Twentieth-Century Catholicism," *South Atlantic Quarterly* 93 (Summer 1994): 547–590.

6. [A. Beiler], *Light in the Shadow of Death*, 126.

7. Letters to the editor, *Family Life*, January 1989, 3.

8. For two accounts and reflections by Amish women on death, see Emma King, *Joys, Sorrows, and Shadows* (Lancaster, PA: Emma King, 1992) and Esther F. Smucker, *Good Night My Son: A Treasure in Heaven* (Morgantown, PA: Olde Springfield Shoppe, 1995). King reflects on the murder of her aunt, and Smucker mourns the accidental death of her son.

9. M. Miller, *Our Heritage, Hope, and Faith*, 319–348, lists the songs, prayers, and scripture readings that are appropriate for funerals.

10. *Unpartheyisches Gesang-Buch: Translations and Lessons* [Impartial Songbook: Translations and Lessons], 2nd ed. (East Earl, PA: Schoolaid, 1997), 171.

11. [A. Beiler], *Light in the Shadow of Death*, 110.

12. "*I Know the Plans I Have for You,*" *Jeremiah 29:11, 16th Annual Sudden Death Reunion, June 20, 2009* (New Holland, PA: n.p.), 25.

13. This quotation and those in the next two paragraphs are from [A. Beiler], *Light in the Shadow of Death*, 97, 230–231, 126, 95.

14. This quotation and the one in the next paragraph are from B. Blank, *The Scriptures Have the Answers*, 172, 174.

Chapter 13: The Things That Matter

1. Sue Bender, *Plain and Simple: A Woman's Journey to the Amish* (San Francisco: HarperOne, 1989), 145.

2. S. Bender, *Plain and Simple*, xii, 146.

3. See, for example, Louise Stoltzfus, *Traces of Wisdom: Amish Women Reflect on Life's Simple Pleasures* (New York: Hyperion, 1998); and Joseph E. Donnermeyer, George M. Kreps, and Marty W. Kreps, *Lessons for Living: A Practical Approach to Daily Life from the Amish Community* (Sugarcreek, OH: Carlisle Press, 1999).

4. Suzanne Woods Fisher, *Amish Peace: Simple Wisdom for a Complicated World* (Grand Rapids, MI: Revell, 2009).

5. S. Fisher, *Amish Peace*, 15.

6. K. Miller and others, "Health Status," 162–171.

7. For one summary, see C. Hurst and D. McConnell, *An Amish Paradox*, 239–245.

8. The research findings reported in this paragraph and the next are from K. Miller and others, "Health Status," 162–171.

9. "The Search for Contentment," *Family Life*, April 1984, 13.

10. Barry Schwartz, *The Paradox of Choice: Why More Is Less* (New York: HarperCollins, 2004), 3. See also Sheena Iyengar, *The Art of Choosing* (New York: Twelve, 2010).

11. S. Fisher, *Amish Peace*, 15–16. Uncle Amos is also cited in J. Donnermeyer, G. Kreps, and M. Kreps, *Lessons for Living*, 175. For the original, see *Small Farmer's Journal* 17, no. 3 (1993): 43–44.

12. This quotation and the one in the next paragraph are from "Teach Your Children to Sing," 18.

13. J. Stoll, "Our Instant Age," 6.

14. "Staff Notes," *Family Life*, November 1994, 5.

REFERENCES

1001 Questions and Answers on the Christian Life. 1992. Aylmer, ON: Pathway Publishers.

Arithmetic Grade Six. 2001. Shipshewana, IN: Study Time Publishers.

Ausbund, Das ist: Etliche schone christlicher Lieder. 1984. Lancaster, PA: Lancaster Press. (First edition in 1564.)

[Beiler, Aaron]. 2008. *Light in the Shadow of Death.* New Holland, PA [840 Peters Road, New Holland, PA 17557]: Aaron Beiler.

Beiler, David. 2009. *True Christianity: A Christian Meditation on the Teachings of Holy Scripture.* Trans. Adelheide Schutzler and Isaac J. Lowry. Parkesburg, PA [3230 Strasburg Road, Parkesburg, PA 19365]: Benuel S. Blank Family.

[Beiler, Joseph F.]. 1982. "Ordnung." *Mennonite Quarterly Review* 56 (4): 382–384.

Bellah, Robert N., Richard Madsen, William M. Sullivan, Ann Swidler, and Steven M. Tipton. 1985. *Habits of the Heart.* San Francisco: Harper Perennial.

Bender, Harold S. 1944. *The Anabaptist Vision.* Scottdale, PA: Herald Press.

Bender, Sue. 1989. *Plain and Simple: A Woman's Journey to the Amish.* San Francisco: HarperOne.

Beyond the Valley: Over 110 Stories of People Who Are Physically Challenged. 2005. Monroe, IN: Hilty Home Sales.

Binford, Hilde E. n.d. "Values and Culture Transmitted Through Music in the Old Order Amish Community," unpublished paper.

[Blank, Ben]. 2001. *The Amazing Story of the Ausbund.* Narvon, PA [205 Churchtown Rd., Narvon, PA 17555]: Benuel S. Blank.

————. 2005. *Creation to Resurrection: A History of Bible Times.* Narvon, PA [205 Churchtown Rd., Narvon, PA 17555]: Benuel S. Blank.

Blank, Ben. 2009. *The Scriptures Have the Answers: Inspirational Writings by Ben Blank*. Parkesburg, PA [3230 Strasburg Road, Parkesburg, PA 19365]: Blank Family.

Botschaft, Die. 1975–. Millersburg, PA: *Die Botschaft* Committee. A weekly newspaper.

Braght, Thieleman J. van. 1968. *Der blutige Schauplatz, oder, Märtyrer-Spiegel der Taufgesinnten, oder, wehrlose Christen, die um des Zeugnisses Jesu, ihres Seligmaches, willen gelitten haben und getötet worden sind, von Christi Zeit an bis auf das Jahr 1660*. Aylmer, ON: Pathway Publishers.

————. 1998. *The Bloody Theatre, or Martyrs Mirror of the Defenseless Christians, Who Baptized Only upon Confession of Faith and Who Suffered and Died for the Testimony of Jesus, Their Saviour, from the Time of Christ to the Year A.D. 1660*. Rev. ed. Scottdale, PA: Herald Press.

Budget, The. 1890–. Sugarcreek, OH: Sugarcreek Budget Publishers. A weekly newspaper.

Complete Writings of Menno Simons, The. 1956. Scottdale, PA: Herald Press.

Connection, The. 2004–. Topeka, IN: The Connection, LLC. A monthly magazine.

Devoted Christian's Prayer Book, A. 1995. Aylmer, ON: Pathway Publishers.

Diary, The. 1969–. Bart, PA: Donald Carpenter. A monthly magazine.

Donnermeyer, Joseph E., George M. Kreps, and Marty W. Kreps. 1999. *Lessons for Living: A Practical Approach to Daily Life from the Amish Community*. Sugarcreek, OH: Carlisle Press.

Doorway to Hope for the Hurting, Struggling and Discouraged, The. n.d. Fort Wayne, IN [P.O. Box 5390, Fort Wayne, IN 46895-5390]: The Sewing Circle.

"Dordrecht Confession of Faith." 2000. In *In Meiner Jugend: A Devotional Reader in German and English*, 8–61. Aylmer, ON: Pathway Publishers.

Durnbaugh, Hedwig T. 1999. "The Amish Singing Style: Theories of Its Origin and Description of Its Singularity." *Pennsylvania Mennonite Heritage* 22 (2): 24–31.

Ernsthafte Christenpflicht, Die. 1996. Lancaster County, PA: Amischen Gemeinden.

Esh, Mrs. Jerre S. [Ruthie], comp. n.d. *A Collection of Treasured Recipes and Poems from the Esh Family*. Christiana, PA [1238 Georgetown Road, Christiana, PA: 17509]: Mrs. Jerre S. [Ruthie] Esh.

Family Life. 1968–. Aylmer, ON: Pathway Publishers. A monthly periodical.

Farming Magazine. 2000–. Mt. Hope, OH: Friends of Agrarians. A quarterly magazine.

Fisher, Suzanne Woods. 2009. *Amish Peace: Simple Wisdom for a Complicated World*. Grand Rapids, MI: Revell.

Garrett, Ottie, ed. 1998. *True Stories of the X-Amish*. Horse Cave, KY: Neu Leben.

Garrett, Ruth Irene, and Rick Farrant. 2003. *Crossing Over: One Woman's Escape from Amish Life*. New York: HarperCollins.

Gross, Leonard, ed. and trans. 1997. *Prayer Book for Earnest Christians*. Scottdale, PA: Herald Press.

Handbuch für Bischof. 1978. Gordonville, PA: Gordonville Print Shop.

Hostetler, John A. 1993. *Amish Society*. 4th ed. Baltimore: Johns Hopkins University Press.

Huntington, Gertrude Enders. 2003. "Health Care." In *The Amish and the State*. 2nd ed., ed. Donald B. Kraybill, 163–190. Baltimore: Johns Hopkins University Press.

Hurst, Charles E., and David L. McConnell. 2010. *An Amish Paradox: Diversity and Change in the World's Largest Amish Community*. Baltimore: Johns Hopkins University Press.

In Meiner Jugend: A Devotional Reader in German and English. 2000. Aylmer, ON: Pathway Publishers.

Indiana Amish Directory: Elkhart, LaGrange, and Noble Counties, 2007. 2007. Middlebury, IN: J. E. Miller.

Iyengar, Sheena. 2010. *The Art of Choosing*. New York: Twelve.

Kline, David. 1997. *Scratching the Woodchuck: Nature on an Amish Farm*. Athens: University of Georgia Press.

———. 2000. "God's Spirit and a Theology for Living." In *Creation and the Environment: An Anabaptist Perspective on a Sustainable World*, ed. Calvin Redekop, 61–69. Baltimore: Johns Hopkins University Press.

Kline, David, Elsie Kline, Richard H. Moore, and Deborah H. Stinner. 1999. "Honouring Creation and Tending the Garden: Amish Views of Bio-diversity." In *Cultural and Spiritual Values of Biodiversity*, ed. Darrell Addison Posey, 305–309. London: Intermediate Technology Publications.

241

King, Emma. 1992. *Joys, Sorrows, and Shadows, by One Who Experienced the Joys, Sorrows, and Shadows*. Lancaster, PA: Emma King.

King, Martin Luther, Jr. 1964. *Why We Can't Wait*. New York: New American Library.

Kraybill, Donald B. 2001. *The Riddle of Amish Culture*. Rev. ed. Baltimore: Johns Hopkins University Press.

————, ed. 2003. *The Amish and the State*. 2nd ed. Baltimore: Johns Hopkins University Press.

Kraybill, Donald B., and Steven M. Nolt. 1995. *Amish Enterprise: From Plows to Profits*. 2nd ed. Baltimore: Johns Hopkins University Press.

Kraybill, Donald B., Steven M. Nolt, and David L. Weaver-Zercher. 2007. *Amish Grace: How Forgiveness Transcended Tragedy*. San Francisco: Jossey-Bass.

Lapp, Mrs. Melvin [Esther], comp. 2005. *Heartland Hymns*. Paradise, PA [313 Wolf Rock Rd., Paradise, PA 17562]: Esther Lapp.

Leith, John H., ed. 1982. *Creeds of the Churches: A Reader in Christian Doctrine from the Bible to the Present*. 3rd ed. Atlanta: John Knox Press.

Louv, Richard. 2008. *Last Child in the Woods: Saving Our Children from Nature-Deficit Disorder*. Rev. ed. Chapel Hill, NC: Algonquin Books of Chapel Hill.

Lucado, Max. 2004. *Six Hours One Friday: Living the Power of the Cross*. Nashville: Thomas Nelson.

McGrath, Alister E. 1997. *An Introduction to Christianity*. Malden, MA: Blackwell Publishers.

Migliore, Daniel L. 2004. *Faith Seeking Understanding: An Introduction to Christian Theology*. 2nd ed. Grand Rapids, MI: Eerdmans.

Miller, Kirk, Berwood Yost, Sean Flaherty, Marianne M. Hillemeier, Gary A. Chase, Carol S. Weisman, and Anne-Marie Dyer. 2007. "Health Status, Health Conditions, and Health Behaviors Among Amish Women: Results from the Central Pennsylvania Women's Health Study (CePAWHS)," *Women's Health Issues* 17:162–171.

Miller, Mary M., comp. 2008. *Our Heritage, Hope, and Faith*. Rev. ed. Topeka, IN [2180 S 900 W, Topeka, IN 46571–9450]: Mary M. Miller.

Neu vermehrtes geistliches Lust Gärtlein frommer Seelen. 2008. Lancaster County, PA: Amischen Gemeinden.

Neue Kinder Lieder: Ein Gesangbuch fur Schulen und Heimaten, Das. 1972. Rev. ed. Aylmer, ON: Pathway Publishers.

Nolt, Steven M. 2003. *A History of the Amish*. Rev. ed. Intercourse, PA: Good Books.

Nolt, Steven M., and Thomas J. Meyers. 2007. *Plain Diversity: Amish Cultures and Identities*. Baltimore: Johns Hopkins University Press.

Olshan, Marc A., and Kimberly D. Schmidt. 1994. "Amish Women and the Feminist Conundrum." In *The Amish Struggle with Modernity*, ed. Donald B. Kraybill and Marc A. Olshan, 215–229. Hanover, NH: University Press of New England.

Orsi, Robert A. 1994. "'Mildred, Is It Fun to Be a Cripple?' The Culture of Suffering in Mid-Twentieth-Century Catholicism." *South Atlantic Quarterly* 93:547–590.

Outley, Nancy Fisher. 1982. "From Amish to Professional and Back Again." In *Perils of Professionalism*, ed. Donald B. Kraybill and Phyllis Pellman Good, 41–49. Scottdale, PA: Herald Press.

Roth, John D., ed. and trans. 2002. *Letters of the Amish Division: A Sourcebook*. 2nd ed. Goshen, IN: Mennonite Historical Society.

"Rules of a Godly Life." 2000. In *In Meiner Jugend: A Devotional Reader in German and English*, 65–103. Aylmer, ON: Pathway Publishers.

Schlabach, Mary, comp. 2007. *Message Mem'ries*. Millersburg, OH [4324 TR 617, Millersburg, OH 44654]: Emanuel and Mary Schlabach.

School Favorites: Around 110 of Our Favorite Songs. 1980. Gordonville, PA: Gordonville Print Shop.

Schwartz, Barry. 2004. *The Paradox of Choice: Why More Is Less*. New York: HarperCollins.

Schwieder, Elmer, and Dorothy Schwieder. 1975. *A Peculiar People: Iowa's Old Order Amish*. Ames: Iowa State University Press.

Scott, Stephen E. 1988. *The Amish Wedding and Other Special Occasions of the Old Order Communities*. Intercourse, PA: Good Books.

Smith, James K. A. 2009. *Desiring the Kingdom: Worship, Worldview, and Cultural Formation*. Grand Rapids, MI: Baker Academic.

Smucker, Esther F. 1995. *Good Night My Son: A Treasure in Heaven*. Morgantown, PA: Olde Springfield Shoppe.

Songs of the Ausbund, Vol. 1. 1998. Millersburg [4292 SR 39, Millersburg, OH 44654]: Ohio Amish Library.

Standards of the Old Order Amish and Old Order Mennonite Parochial and Vocational Schools of Pennsylvania. 1988. Old Order Book Society. Reprint. Gordonville, PA: Gordonville Print Shop, 2006.

Stevick, Pauline. 2006. *Beyond the Plain and Simple: A Patchwork of Amish Lives*. Kent, OH: Kent State University Press.

Stevick, Richard A. 2007. *Growing Up Amish: The Teenage Years*. Baltimore: Johns Hopkins University Press.

[Stoll, Elmo]. 2008. *Strangers and Pilgrims: Why We Live Simply*. Aylmer, ON: Pathway Publishers.

Stoltzfus, Louise. 1998. *Traces of Wisdom: Amish Women Reflect on Life's Simple Pleasures*. New York: Hyperion.

Stoltzfus, Samuel S. 2008. "Going in with the Boys," *Pennsylvania Mennonite Heritage* 31 (1): 31–32.

Strobel, Lee. 1998. *The Case for Christ: A Journalist's Personal Investigation of the Evidence for Jesus*. Grand Rapids, MI: Zondervan.

Taylor, Charles. 2004. *Modern Social Imaginaries*. Durham, NC: Duke University Press.

Umble, Diane Zimmerman, and David L. Weaver-Zercher, eds. 2008. *The Amish and the Media*. Baltimore: Johns Hopkins University Press.

Unpartheyisches Gesang-Buch: Translations and Lessons. 1997. 2nd ed. East Earl, PA: Schoolaid.

Wagler, David. n.d. *Are All Things Lawful?* Aylmer, ON: Pathway Publishers.

Wallmann, Jeffrey M. 1999. *The Western: Parables of the American Dream*. Lubbock: Texas Tech University Press.

Warren, Rick. 2002. *The Purpose Driven Life: What on Earth Am I Here For?* Grand Rapids, MI.: Zondervan.

Weaver-Zercher, David L. 2001. *The Amish in the American Imagination*. Baltimore: Johns Hopkins University Press.

Writings of David A. Troyer, The. 1998. Aylmer, ON: Pathway Publishers.

Yoder, John H., ed. and trans. 1977. *The Schleitheim Confession*. Scottdale, PA: Herald Press.

Yoder, Paton. 1991. *Tradition and Transition: Amish Mennonites and Old Order Amish, 1800–1900*. Scottdale, PA: Herald Press.

Yoder, Sarah Jean. 1995. *Benjie, the In-Between Boy*. Aylmer, ON: Pathway Publishers.

Pathway Publishers is an Amish-owned publisher. Items in the references published by Pathway as well as other books from its annual catalog can be obtained by writing to Pathway Publishers, Route 4, Aylmer, Ontario N5H 2R3 Canada.

THE AUTHORS

DONALD B. KRAYBILL is distinguished professor and senior fellow at the Young Center for Anabaptist and Pietist Studies at Elizabethtown College in Elizabethtown, Pennsylvania. He has studied and published on numerous Anabaptist communities in North America. His books include *The Riddle of Amish Culture* (rev. ed., 2001), *The Amish and the State*, an edited collection (rev. ed., 2003), and *Concise Encyclopedia of Amish, Brethren, Hutterites, and Mennonites* (2010), all published by Johns Hopkins University Press.

STEVEN M. NOLT is professor of history at Goshen College in Goshen, Indiana. He has studied Amish history and culture across many settlements. His books include *A History of the Amish* (rev. ed., Good Books, 2003), *Amish Enterprise: From Plows to Profits* (2nd ed., with Donald B. Kraybill, Johns Hopkins University Press, 2004), and *Plain Diversity: Amish Cultures and Identities* (with Thomas J. Meyers, Johns Hopkins University Press, 2007).

DAVID L. WEAVER-ZERCHER is professor of American religious history at Messiah College in Grantham, Pennsylvania. He has written extensively on mainstream Americans' interest in and perceptions of the Amish. His books include *The Amish in the American Imagination* (Johns Hopkins University Press, 2001) and two edited volumes, *Writing the Amish: The Worlds of John A. Hostetler* (Pennsylvania State University Press, 2005), and *The Amish and the Media* (with Diane Zimmerman Umble, Johns Hopkins University Press, 2008).

INDEX